INSTAGRAM HACKS 2020

Influencer Marketing Made Easy While Growing a Brand and Advertising your Business

Aiden Winters

Table of Contents

Introduction

Boomerang.   Insta Stories. Polls. Live Videos.

If you recognized any of the words above, then you are aware of one of the most popular social media platforms on the planet; Instagram.

If you recognized all the words mentioned in the first line, then look at you, you Instagram maestro!

According to the Global Web Index, Instagram is the fifth highest social media platform in terms of members and registered users. However, I think Instagram might have to move up a few paces. You see, the other four platforms on the list are the below (in the order of their ranking):

- Facebook

- YouTube

- Facebook Messenger

- WhatsApp

- Instagram

Obviously, Facebook has three of its brands on the list. That does not seem fair. So, if you were to combine all Facebook products into a single ranking spot, then the list would look something like this:

- Facebook, Facebook Messengers, WhatsApp, and Instagram

- YouTube

But we are still going to have to break down the statistics per platform in order to maintain accuracy. And hence, Instagram gets fifth place.

That is no small feat and comes with quite a lot of incredible statistics. Here are just a few of them:

- Over 1 billion people log into Instagram and use the platform every month. Out of that staggering number of users, nearly 500 million people logged are using the platform every day!

- Do you think the majority of the users are from the U.S.? Think again. Nearly 88% of the platform's users are located in international boundaries. Want to promote your stuff in countries like Brazil, Indonesia, Japan, Turkey, and India? Heck, you just need an Instagram account.

- In 2016, it was recorded that there were 96 million posts per day on the platform. That is nearly 35 billion posts in a year. That means every person on the planet had to post at least 5 posts every day! I don't even upload 5 posts a week!

- There have been at least 80% increase in the video uploads on a yearly basis.

- If you are a business, then you might like this fact: over 71% of businesses in the U.S. use Instagram. And why is that? Well, it is because...

- ...nearly 60% of Instagram users discover new products

on the platform. That becomes important when you understand the fact that...

- ...Instagram has an interaction rate of 2.2%. While that might sound like a lot, it is a significant stat for marketers. How significant? Let's say that the interaction rate on Instagram is higher than any platform, including Facebook. Oh yeah, that big.

But these are just some of the reasons why you should be heading over to this platform to market your business.

That is right.

In today's world of connectivity, not using a social media platform to reach out to people is not just a missed opportunity; it might very well be a marketing blunder. With just a free account, you have so many opportunities and possibilities. Want to spend a little to increase your reach? Sure, you can. And you won't be doing it by reaching out to an arbitrary number of people. It is not like posting a billboard on the highway and making a guess on the number of people who might have seen your marketing efforts.

On Instagram, you are given real numbers. You have real statistics. You have the power to use these numbers to know exactly what idea, visual, and content works. Need to know how many people commented on your post? You got it. Want to respond to your audience. Of course, you can!

As the years go by, Instagram is still popular among various brands, celebrities, social influencers, and businesses. It is still strong and does not show signs of slowing down. And, as the years go by, Instagram has become a powerful marketing tool. Sure, you can still share pictures of your friends and family or that time you went to Bali and saw the Monkey Temple. You can still show pictures of your birthdays and accomplishments. However, if you are a brand or business looking for an opportunity (and I say 'brand' to denote individuals since each individual is creating a brand of his or her own on the platform), unless you are actively engaging on Instagram, you are missing out on the opportunities presented by the platform. There is so much you can accomplish and many ways to do it. Instagram is a valuable tool, that much is certain. But it has now evolved to be a potent force in marketing.

In fact, let's try to look at some stats about Instagram, showing how advertisers can use the platform to increase their exposure. (All statistics mentioned below are for 2019.)

- Instagram has 1 billion active monthly users.

- After Facebook, Instagram is the most engaged network.

- Instagram users spend an average of 53 minutes a day on the platform!

With all of these stats, it's easy to see why the platform is growing in popularity among influencers, brands, and businesses.

So, let us get right down to it and delve into the world of #Instagram.

Chapter 1:
Why Instagram and How to Get Started Using the Platform

Humans are visual creatures. According to the Social Science Research Network, nearly 65 percent of human beings are visual learners. Which is why the visual-heavy platform of Instagram is perfect for reaching create a more concrete impression in the minds of the people.

Want to know something really cool? When people hear something, only 3% of their brain is engaged. And when they see something? Well, that percentage shoots up to 30%!

There is a lot of significance there (and a lot of opportunities). When it comes to Instagram, nearly all of your content is visual based. Which is why a significant percentage of the population can relate with your content as you are showing them what you would like to communicate. This, in turn, creates a visual identity for you and your profile. People know the kind of content to expect from you. Those who enjoy your content begin following you (more on followers in the next section) and they, in turn, promote your content to other people. Pretty soon, you have a fairly decent sized audience growing along with you.

This visual storytelling ability of Instagram is what defines the platform. It's what makes Instagram a unique app that is attracting quite a number of people (billions, in fact).

So, What Exactly Is Instagram?

Instagram is a popular free social media application which allows users to share pictures and videos. As an online mobile and web-based social networking service app, Instagram permits users to take photos, shoot videos and share them with friends on a range of other social media platforms, including Facebook, Twitter, and Flickr.

It is available for download mainly on Apple iOS, Android and Windows mobile devices. You can open the app using any web browser from a desktop computer, but you are limited to simply viewing your collection of photos and videos. You cannot capture or upload any media on Instagram using your PC browser.

On the app, Instagram users can take photos or videos to upload, and then share them with their followers or with a select few friends. In the same manner, users can also view, comment, or like posts and videos shared by their followers and friends on Instagram. Instagram is restricted to persons who are 13 years old and above.

Why the heavy reliance on mobile? According to Statista, internet traffic from mobile devices was 50 percent. Experts predict that this percentage will rise tremendously by 2020. This is why businesses increasingly seek to target mobile users or have a separate marketing budget to target mobile users. In the U.S. alone, mobile will take up 86% of the digital marketing efforts of businesses between 2017 and 2022.

The Origin Story: Who Created Instagram?

Although originally developed by two independent developers and Stanford University graduates Kevin Systrom and Mike

Krieger, Instagram has since been acquired by Facebook (for a whopping $1 billion, which could very well be the GDP of a country). Instagram was founded in 2010 and had been used by more than 200 million people across the globe by the time it was acquired in 2012.

The platform caters to a diverse demographic. You have sports personalities and actors on the platform. You have politicians, activists, and scientists spreading messages on Instagram. You even have brands and the general public using the platform to share their ideas, interests, and activities.

How Does Instagram Work?

Instagram is a social media app that is easy to use, has a friendly interface, and is open to a large number of users. Basically, most of the features that people look for in an app.

It also comes with a capacity for users to link up and share photos and video content across major social media platforms, including Facebook and Twitter. The process of having Instagram begins by creating a personal profile. Once you have created your profile, you are going to go through the usual procedure of uploading your profile image, create a little blurb about you in your bio, and all the little actions to complete your profile.

After the acquisition by Facebook, signing up onto the platform has become much easier if you have an existing Facebook account. You can easily link it to your account on Facebook, and it will use all of your information on Facebook to complete your account on Instagram.

Instagram emphasizes mobile use and visual sharing. Once you take a picture, Instagram filters allow you to transform and edit the image to suit your taste and preferences. In short, you have a compact (and an extremely rudimentary) form of a Photoshop-like editing feature provided to you by Instagram.

Instagram gives users the capacity to use numerous filters that basically add unique tints and visual effects to the images and videos. With unique names for filters such as Valencia, Clarendon, and Juno among a host of others, Instagram provides also aids the user to recognize these filters instantly when they want to use them next. Want to add a vintage effect to your images? Sure, you have the Gingham filter to help you with that. Want to add an intense look where the center of the image is the main focus? Just apply the Lo-Fi filter.

Like Twitter and Facebook, Instagram is not limited to the sharing of photos and videos alone. It allows users to connect and interact with other users on the platform. It also has features which will enable you to follow people or allow them to follow you. You can also like or tag a photo or video content. In this same manner, Instagram offers an incredible opportunity for users to comment on content. You can have a private message with a follower. You can also save photos shared on the platform.

For a business, this becomes vital because they are provided a platform to share visual ideas, stories, messages, and promotions.

What Makes Instagram Great?

One of Instagram's appeals is that it provides unique ways to express yourself and connect with people based on your interests. It is not just about uploading images to a platform. Heck, one can do that with social media portals like Facebook and Twitter.

You can create an online community with the media and

messages you create on Instagram. In fact, your profile becomes part of an online sharing community. It allows people to enjoy your content while you, in turn, respond to theirs.

It creates a circle of interaction where the circle keeps expanding based on the number of people you add to your community. And where there is community, there is loyalty. If your content is accepted and liked by enough people or on a frequent basis, then you can create a number of ardent followers of your content.

So how does Instagram allow people to create all of the fantastic content that create communities, loyal followers, and incredible engagement?

It does so by its ever-growing features.

Here are some of them.

Instagram Questions

Instagram Questions is one of the newly introduced features of Instagram. This feature allows Instagram users to supply relevant answers to questions posed by their followers. You can locate this feature in the sticker drawer. If you are unable to find it there, you need to update to the latest version of the software.

Anyone who answers a particular question has their profile open to followers and other users. However, the person who asks the question will not be shown to the responder. So, while there's no anonymity about the person who answers a question, the person who asks, even though he or she gets a notification when you respond to the question, will not be shown as having asked the question.

This creates an interesting concept. People enjoy the power of anonymity. It allows them to ask questions without worrying about revealing their identity. Because they can be anonymous, they can have some honest interactions with the user. This, in turn, allows people and businesses to understand how to reach out to their audience better.

Instagram Direct

Instagram Direct is one of those fantastic features that clearly distinguishes Instagram from many other social networking platforms. With this feature, users from their newsfeed can share videos, images, hashtag locations, profiles, and pages with as much as 15 people. You will also be able to have private conversations and leave comments on stories using this feature. If you come across something funny or important on your feed and would like to share with a friend or loved one, you can equally do so using this feature.

The Instagram Direct menu can be easily accessed on the app. It is located in the top right-hand part of the application via the inbox icon.

Instagram Stories

Another great feature of Instagram is Instagram Stories. With this feature, users are allowed to share a collection of select photos or video content into a single story. Instagram Stories takes the best aspects of both the WhatsApp and Snapchat stories to create an enhanced experience with the Story feature. They strictly follow the privacy setting policy, which guides user's Instagram Profile. In other words, when you post a story, it can only be seen by those who follow you. No other person will be able to access or view it.

Augmented Reality

Augmented reality? Sounds brilliant and exciting, doesn't it?!

Yes, it is and the platform is testing how to effectively use augmented reality. It wants to provide its users with much more creative options. But what is augmented reality? Is it similar to virtual reality?

You could say that. One of the unique things about augmented reality is that you can project things onto the landscape using the device. For example, let's say that you use your phone camera to look at a road. Augmented reality allows you to create images and pictures on the road that will appear on the phone's camera. You could see a giant dragon land on the road or watch other animations. Of course, everything is happening on your device, but it is still fun to play around with isn't it? Imagine you are on your next holiday and you see something awesome and you just have to take a video of it. Why use a regular video when you can modify it with awesome animations?

This becomes truly useful for businesses and brands who can showcase their products in 3D format or actually give a demonstration of the product in action. The potential that the feature provides puts Instagram on another level; one that sets it apart from other social media platforms.

In fact, one of the best parts about the augmented reality software is that you can try out different products and check out how they look on you, for example. Turn your camera to face yourself and choose the sunglasses you would like to try on. If you are satisfied with the look, go ahead and make the purchase. Clothing and accessories are also available for trying out.

When the software rolls out completely, there will be many features for people to try out. For example, let's assume that you are a store that sells plants and other decorative items for homes. Now the user can simply point the camera at a shelf or table and choose the potted plant that he or she would like to place there. Augmented reality will then place the object there, in 3D. This gives the user a better impression of what the object will look like in their home. In other words, they can use your products in an actual demonstration.

Product Launch Reminders

See what I mean by the fact that Instagram is improving its marketing efforts? With the product launch feature, you can actually create a reminder option that will automatically appear on the feeds of your users.

This is a unique feature that has incredible potential for businesses that are focused on selling physical goods through the social media platform. It allows you businesses to display their products and their features or give a small teaser about the product to the audience. This raises the excitement and anticipation level of your audience. Once created, your launch date can be displayed.

Now here is the best part. You can set the launch date, down to the hour and minute. When the day and hour approaches, your audience will receive a push notification, which then takes them to the post and Instagram story. This form of marketing is much better than many traditional methods or marketing.

Think about it this way. You spend thousands – maybe tens of thousands – of dollars on marketing and letting people know that a product is going to arrive in the market soon. Once the product has been released, you might have to spend even more on advertisement. So why not take a cheaper option that allows you to reach far more people and give them a linked notification when the product is released? In fact, you can also target people around the world who are on the platform with the additional audience targeting features.

Direct Messaging App

By now, you know that Facebook has its own messaging app. The feature is pretty convenient for people who would like to communicate with each other or reach out to certain people.

What if I told you that Instagram has that feature as well?

But you might wonder, why is Instagram releasing a direct messaging app?

The short answer is to improve marketing.

You can use Facebook to promote products and services in its messaging app. There are many people who actually go on Facebook only to chat with their friends and family. This was noticed by the social media giant. They launched an app that helps people simply communicate with each other without actually going on the social media platform. This gave them greater opportunities to send advertisements to people even when they are not on the platform. Pretty smart isn't it?

Now Instagram is going to use the same idea. They understand that sometimes people do not actually come to the platform to check out their feed. Rather, they simply want to communicate with people and friends. With a separate messaging app, people can use this feature, and advertisers can reach more people. It's a win-win situation.

Cool Features. But Why Are Businesses Using The Platform?

According to Sprout Social, Instagram is predicted to take up nearly a quarter of all of Facebook's ad revenue by the end of 2019.

Why is there such a rapid growth of the platform? Why are more and more businesses flocking to Instagram to promote their products and services or create their brand identity?

There is a lot that a business can gain by using Instagram apart from just uploading photos and videos to the public. The platform is not just used for uploading photos and videos from people who would like to show glimpses of their lives.

People who buy into this false impression believe that Instagram is not intended for serious minded businesspeople. This is wrong and completely false. Here are a few of the ways in which Instagram is helping businesses.

Visual + Copy = A Marketers Dream Come True

We already established that visuals create an incredible impact in the minds of the viewers. But Instagram allows businesses to combine great visuals and catchy copy.

You can provoke an emotion. You can ask a question. You can tell a wonderful story. There are so many ways you can engage with your audience that is not possible using flyers, posters, billboards, and other traditional forms of marketing. The way in which you create your marketing is only limited to your imagination, and that is not an exaggeration.

At this point, it is not an understatement to say that if you don't have your business on Instagram yet, you are missing out on opportunities.

You have the power to create incredible visuals through images and video. You can be funny. You can be thought-provoking. You can be serious about topics. Instagram allows you to develop your persona and gain an audience for it.

There's Free Advertising

Who doesn't love free stuff?

Think of it this way; you spend hundreds of thousands of dollars on billboards.

You spend zero dollars on Instagram.

For businesses, the platform allows them to use a profitable area where they can minimize expenditure and maximize effectiveness.

Advertising can be one of the most cash-intensive aspects of a business that, if not careful enough with, could sink capital with little or no gain.

Instagram has come to reduce that burden off you. The platform offers free advertising, in which case, you can display your services and products without paying a dime. You can make use of all its features, including live streaming your interactions or services to your followers and letting your followers see the incredible things you're doing. This way, you're gaining exposure and selling your brand to both existing and potential customers. You can even upload pictures and videos of past activities of your company and let users and followers follow, like, or comment on the post — all of this you do without committing a penny.

Frequency

Traditional advertising methods are expensive. You cannot create a new ad every day!

But with Instagram, you definitely can. Everyday.

The platform is free. How you utilize it is entirely up to you. Do you have so many products that you would like to talk about (for example, your business could be a clothing boutique)? Then you might want your audience to see your products frequently. You want to show them how diverse your offerings are.

Do you have a car showroom? Then perhaps you may not want to publish an ad on Instagram every day. You might choose to do it every week to allow for each of the cars in your showroom to be under the spotlight.

This degree of flexibility is what makes Instagram truly appealing. Businesses have the option to market themselves at a rate that is comfortable to them.

Increase Your Sales Margin

When Instagram realized the potential it could provide to businesses, it ramped up the number of tools and features it offered businesses. For instance, it recently introduced shoppable posts that allow businesses to post their products with price, description, and a "shop now" button. The button can direct audiences to a specific online destination, such as a product page or a registration form, depending on what the business is aiming to achieve. This encourages users to enter the destination and perform an action that the business would like them to perform. In that case, the business can attract larger than the average number of customers and thus increase sales and profit margin.

Attract Traffic to Your Blog or Website

Again, Instagram is a platform that drives traffic to your blog or website. Using photos and videos to catch follower's attention, you're sure of building an increased community of people who will continue to demand your service over and over again. It's a fact that Instagram drives more engaged traffic to your blog or site than any other social media channel. The number of minutes people spend on Instagram far outweighs those spend on other platforms such as Facebook, Pinterest, YouTube, Reddit, or Twitter.

Instagram Is a Great Source of UGC

User Generated content is a kind of content that has been developed by individuals who love your brand without any payment. These could range from video, images, text, or any other content that users utilize in promoting the brand without any input from the brand itself.

With the fast pace at which social media is growing, it's becoming challenging to keep engaging followers with new content daily. You've got to generate content that can instantly grab the attention of the users. Instagram is the perfect source where you can derive the best content that will make your business stay relevant and attractive to customers. In that way, Instagram is achieving multiple things for you at the same time.

Conversation Gets Interesting With a Lot of Characters

What do I mean by a lot? On that note, just what do I mean by characters?

By characters, I am referring to the number of letters, numbers, and spaces that you can use to convey your message. Instagram provides you with the ability to use up to 2,200 characters for your post.

Imagine you start a conversation with a customer and feel the need to convey a lengthy piece of information, you can do so with relative ease. You can pass on the information you want via a single post without having to spend so much time splitting it via different posts. Through a single post, your customers are going to understand everything they would like to know about your product or service.

Your Business Goes On Instagram Ahead Of You

One other beautiful thing about Instagram is that you can have your business already online on Instagram. This is done with the presence of your customers who are already using the platform. This means that someone who has used your products or services is already talking to Instagram users about your brand. This can happen in many ways. For instance, a customer goes to your store, takes a snapshot right in front of it, uploads and shares it on Instagram with a clear logo of your company conspicuously standing in the background of the photo. The customer could also hashtag your company with their posts and make mention of it while sharing the photos or videos.

Wait, what are hashtags?

Well, think of hashtags as a space to communicate about a specific topic. If you use a particular hashtag, then your post gets shown under that hashtag. So, let us understand this by an example. If you upload a post about cats, then you are probably going to use hashtags such as #CuteCats, #CatsAreTheBest or

#ILoveCatsVeryMuchThatIWantToCreateAnIslandForThemA
ndWatchThemMultiply.

Okay, maybe not the last option. But you get the picture.

Now, every time somebody creates a post on Instagram and
uses the #CuteCats hashtag, their post gets listed in a sub-page
under that hashtag. In many ways, hashtags are a way to collect
media and content that share a common theme.

So how does this affect your business?

Time for another example.

Let us assume that you have a business selling the world's first
double-espresso ice chocolate vanilla essence white mocha
Caribbean bean Frappuccino. We might need to work on the
name.

So, let us say that you are selling this hard-to-remember
Frappuccino and your customers absolutely love it. What they
are going to do is take a picture of their experience, upload it on
Instagram, and hashtag your business.

Bam. Instant exposure. And you did not even have to spend a
dime.

But here is the problem. All that exposure will not do you any
favors if you do not have an account on Instagram. That is
because you can actually view the content created by your
customers and respond to them. You begin creating
conversations. You increase engagement. Eventually, you
create brand loyalty, and that means more customers.

All this for free.

Isn't that something you would love to take advantage of?

It's not just the young folks or those willing to expose themselves to the world that Instagram is meant for. It is for your business growth; it is for its exposure, its expansion, its exposure, its visibility, its profit margin, and its sales increase.

You Can Reach The Right Audience

Brazil. Japan. China. Italy.

No, I am not listing down all the countries I have visited. I am talking about finding a market that fits your needs.

Is your business part of the fashion industry and you would like to target women between the ages of 18 and 35 in the country of France? You can.

Do you manufacturer the latest tech and gadgets and you would like to target men in the UK aged between 18 to 40? You can.

Whatever your goals, you can find a customer base on Instagram. You can connect with people not just within your region, but also in international territories. This allows you to scale your business in ways that you might not have imagined.

Think about it. If you are a software producer, then you can actually promote your product anywhere in the world. All customers might need to do is head over to your website and download your software. Maybe you might receive a strong customer base in China.

But I wonder. Where can we find a platform that allows you to promote for free while using multiple visual mediums and simultaneously targeting the type of audiences you would like?

Oh right.

Instagram.

You Can Reach Customers On Different Channels Simultaneously

Today's technology has made it possible to operate more than one channel of application. It could be Twitter, Instagram, Facebook, LinkedIn, the official brand website, and Snapchat. Just because you operate one or two of these applications does not limit your ability to operate across all available channels. The important thing, however, is to be accurately aware of who your target audience is and how you can reach them. It is a waste of time and money if these available channels are not properly managed. However, there is a considerable advantage of operating these channels simultaneously: it helps connect your customers to you one way or another. There are instances where some people come across your business solely through your web page, and if they see displayed pictures of your Instagram account on your page, they are likely to visit your Instagram page too. The advantage of this is that they are likely to visit your page on Instagram more often than if your business page was limited to just your website. Another possibility is when a potential customer who visits your Instagram account also accesses your website via a link you leave on the platform and confirms that your company has what they need.

Instagram allows you to reach clients on various channels simultaneously. In turn, this widens the scope of available audiences for the business and, as a result, increases sales. Since your target audience might be more active on one social media platform than the other, it presents the opportunity for high engagement with potential customers and clients from across various platforms.

Instagram Offers You Lots Of Tools To Monitor Success

It is quite easy to be carried away with the numbers of followers and likes on an Instagram page. It is a fact that the numbers of likes and followers do not translate to the success of a business. A business is considered successful through the number of sales made, the commitment of customers, and the increase in more customers. The question then is, how do you closely monitor your business's success rate on Instagram?

The platform makes it easy by providing you with useful tools for analytics to help determine which content displayed was most widely responded to by customers. An example of this is Instagram Insights, which Instagram offers to business accounts free of charge.

It Helps Your Brand Develop Trust And Personality With Clients

The general perspective of a company is that it is a separate entity from a person and, as such, a face or name is usually not attached to it. Instagram has dramatically helped bridge that gap. The application enables your customers to view your products in a more relaxed and informal way. Features such as Instagram Stories create a connection between the seller and the buyers, resulting in a personal sense and feel to your business. The comments sections also give customers the opportunity to review products without any form of restrictions. With all of these combined, Instagram adds a valuable factor of personality to your company or business that inevitably leads to trust. Trust results in constant feedback and great referrals.

It Is Visual

People are automatically attracted to what they see (remember the stats we provided before). Instagram creates visuals of company content and makes it accessible to millions and thousands of people. The main feature of Instagram is the exclusivity of pictures and videos. Unlike some social media platforms that focus on the written word, such as LinkedIn, Instagram allows you to show a creative picture of what your products can offer. Since people are more drawn to pictures than text, Instagram presents a perfect marketing tool for your company to explore. Once creative content is posted, it can be reposted by other people who either relate with it or love the concept. It presents an opportunity to reflect and emphasize the soul of a business.

How to Create a Business Instagram Account

Creating an Instagram business account is a straightforward process. The steps below cover how you can do this without hassle.

- **Step 1** - Download the application. If you are using an Apple Phone, go on Apple Store and click GET. If you are using an Android phone, go to the Google Play store. If it is a windows phone, go to Windows App Stores to download the app. The app is not limited to just phones; it can be downloaded on computers or tablets too. However, it is mostly advised to use on a mobile phone, as some of the features might need a special plug-in order to work on a PC or a laptop.

- **Step 2** - Create An Account. You have the option of signing in with your e-mail account or your mobile number. Use whichever you consider stress free. Then you are also given the option to link your Facebook account to your Instagram account. This is advisable because it connects the audience of your Facebook account to your Instagram Profile and also makes it possible to share the same displayed pictures on Facebook too.

How do you link your accounts? Let's find out below.

It is vital to remember that the Facebook Page you are linking with your Instagram page is a business account page and not a personal profile page. On the other hand, if you want your customers to have a peek into the personal life of the person behind the brand, then you could equally link your personal profile page. However, I would recommend using a business page for the purpose of linking accounts.

To begin, start by clicking your profile icon, click and scroll to the beginning of the right side of the page, then click on setting. Next, scroll until you find the command that tells you to switch to the business profile, keep scrolling until see the connect to Facebook, after that click on the choose a page command, then change it to Public, then click on OK. Instagram will seek your go-ahead to manage your Facebook account, click on Next.

- **Step 4-** The next course of action is to fill your data in on the provided columns. Fill the correct information in, and once you are through, click on the done button.

- **Step 5 -** At this point, you are ready to create your business profile. Various types of businesses will be listed below, which include music, websites, and blogs, local businesses, sports, brands, and products. You are advised to pick the best category that suits your business and your products. To aid an easy search, choose a related subcategory – and afterward, click on the button next.

- **Step 6** - Now, you have the option of editing your profile to best suit your needs. This is where you add your picture or your company's logo. As you are working with your business, the ideal move would be to add your logo to your profile. You will also be able to fill in the bio of your company. You have just 150 characters to play with, so make sure you are creating a bio that makes an impact. Consider the following options:

  - State what your core values are and what you stand for. This is sort of a cover note to your potential clients, who want to know what you are all about and what you do.

  - Describe your company in a captivating technique. Perhaps you could single out your Unique Selling Points (or USPs) and highlight them. For example, you could be serving all-natural yogurt. Let that be what you focus on in your bio.

  - Be unique and creative. Add humor if you would like to. However, if you are a non-profit organization dealing with situations like poverty and unemployment, then humor might not be something you should adopt. However, that does not mean you cannot be creative. Check out this profile bio for World Bicycle Relief, a non-profit organization that supplies bicycles to the poorer areas in Africa so that people can commute to jobs, work, or simply use the bicycles for travel:

With a bicycle, everything changes. #racingthesun

- The above bio provides the audience with a powerful statement. But the company did not simply decide to use any phrase. They wanted to create an impact. World Bicycle Relief has said more in just five words than many fail to communicate in five paragraphs. And they did that with a flair of creativity.

- **Step 7 -** Now that you are set, invite your contacts. The app presents an opportunity to invite your followers or friends and family on Facebook to follow you on Instagram, and it also extends to other networks like LinkedIn, Yahoo, Twitter, or Gmail. All you have to do is to click on the Invite friends option. If you make use of the invite your friends on Facebook option, it will automatically send messages to your customers on Facebook that you have currently signed up on Instagram. That way, you get followers without stressing much. If you are an up-and-coming business, then this feature is extremely useful as it allows you to use people you know to market your business. If you are an existing business, then perhaps you might not have to focus on this step as you are probably aiming to target your customers directly.

- **Step 8 -** Finally, you are ready to start uploading your posts! At this point, you want to show people what your company represents. You can create creative content that attracts customers to your page. In the beginning, it might seem complicated and a bit overwhelming but remember you want to share your products to the world. It consistently helps to create content. You can also make sure you make use of every available feature on Instagram to share your experiences. Such as Instagram Stories, Highlights, and Direct Messages from your customers. Do not be rigid. Remember that you are aiming to create a personal and long-lasting relationship with your customers.

Score a Goal! Having the Right Goal for Your Instagram

Time for a truth pill; just because you have so many features on Instagram, it does not mean that you are going to be able to succeed easily.

Just like any other marketing campaign, you will need a goal in order to make your strategies effective.

But just how can you determine what goals are right for you? Well, here are a few tips for you to follow:

Tip#1

Let's get started with the foundation for your goals and probably one of the most important questions you are going to be asking yourself: what are you planning to achieve on Instagram? What is the objective of your brand for using a platform like Instagram?

Those seem like rather broad questions, so let us simplify them further so that it makes it easier for you to approach your goal-making process.

- What can Instagram provide you with that you cannot gain from other platforms?

- Who is your target audience? Where are they located? What do they like and how active are they?

- How can you combine Instagram with other marketing tools that are part of your digital marketing strategy? Your digital marketing strategy is all the components that are part of your online presence, such as your website, Google advertising, social media advertising, online blogs, podcasts, and more. You should try and see how you can integrate Instagram into these strategies. For example: if you have a website, then you are first going to add Instagram icons on your homepage so that people can discover your Instagram profile. If you are creating regular podcasts online, then you might mention your Instagram in your podcasts. These are just some of the ways in which you can create awareness or grow your Instagram profile effectively.

Tip #2

You should now focus on developing a content strategy.

You cannot just post anything you feel like on Instagram, add a few hashtags, and hope that your marketing strategies work.

Let us take an example.

If you have a restaurant, then simply posting images of your food is going to get old and outdated real fast. People are going to see the same food shot in different camera angles or under different filters.

So, what can you do?

Let's see if we can create a content strategy together.

The first thing you have to do is evaluate your restaurant. What is its theme? Is it a seafood restaurant? Are you focused on Italian cuisine? Do you serve Japanese food?

Next, do you have a special way to cook certain dishes? Do you have live cooking stations? Think of the unique features of your restaurant.

Then focus on the location of your restaurant. What is so unique about where your restaurant is located?

Then finally, look at all the latest trends when it comes to food. Check out upcoming events, popular news, and local updates.

Collect all the information together, and you should have a content strategy like the one below:

Type of Post	Details
Images	Images of your food. Pictures of the customers sharing a wonderful moment with your staff. Your customers are doing something funny/spontaneous/awesome that you would like to share.
Video	Videos of your restaurant interior. Your staff is serving guests. If possible, your guests are responding to the food they enjoyed in your restaurant.

Images and Videos	What makes your location unique? Is there a nearby landmark that is quite popular? Perhaps a piece of information nobody knew about the area? This is an interesting way not just to create an engaging content but also show people where you are located. Instead of just saying, "hey, look! I am here!" you are instead saying, "Hey look at this awesome thing you need to know about where I am located."
Images and Videos	Was there a movie shooting taking place in your neighborhood? Talk about it! Tell people to meet some great cast while enjoying your food! Was there a New Year's event near your location? Make sure people know about it and let them know that you have the right stuff for a little hangover!

See what we did there? By simply focusing on creating a content strategy, we just added so many unique ways to express ourselves. So, make sure that you create a content strategy for yourself, so you can separate yourself from your competitors.

Tip #3

Once you have figured out your content strategy, you have to see how often you would like to post on Instagram. It is not just a matter of simply thinking that you are going to publish one image on one video every day. You have a business to run after all! What are you planning to do to balance your business activities and marketing activities?

Would it benefit you if you had a weekly strategy? You could publish content perhaps thrice a week, allowing you to have enough time to come up with creative content and yet not suffer burnout because you have been spending so many hours stressing about your Instagram content!

Tip #4

Look for branded hashtags. These are hashtags that are currently trending. For example, the #GetTogetherAlready hashtag was trending in late 2019. Other businesses, brands, influencers, and celebrities took the opportunity to jump in on the popularity of the hashtag and then use it to their advantage. Soon, you had the likes of popular actor Jean Claude Van Damme promoting products using that hashtag.

Always keep a lookout for trending subjects to talk about. If the Oscars are closing, you might begin to notice certain hashtags related to the event. Try to create a marketing campaign revolving around that hashtag.

But this tip comes with a caveat. Try to stay away from hashtags that address politics, religion, race, gender, and other such issues. Unless you plan to chip in a positive message to support some of the causes in the world, do not use these types of hashtags simply for marketing purposes. Your audience might notice that and might even oppose your marketing campaigns as being too insensitive to the cause. Even though that might not have been your intention.

You will always find hashtags that are safe to use. Take advantage of them.

Another important point to note is that you should not use a hashtag if you do not have a strong marketing campaign that incorporates the theme of the hashtag. For example, if you see a hashtag such as #DogsRule, then you cannot use it to promote your new line of shirts without any reference to dogs. Your audience will quickly catch on to that.

Tip #5

Create a color palette and brand theme. Nowadays, brands and businesses are taking every opportunity that they can get to stand out from the competition. This means that they want to be as unique as possible. But why does it matter? Why do businesses want to create their own theme?

With so many brands and entities already on Instagram, businesses need to find new ways to create a lasting impression in the minds of their users and audience. Adding a color theme or color palette allows users to identify the business easily.

At the same time, a brand theme can bring a sense of cohesiveness to your page. It makes your account look clean and reduces visual chaos. It allows you to organize your media. Essentially, you are making sure that your brand is represented properly on the platform.

Picking the Ideal Instagram Name

In the technology-driven business world of today, when it

comes to social media, having a name that is catchy and quickly picked up by the various internet search engines is of paramount importance. The name you give your social media page bears some similarity to a website link nowadays.

I am not asking you to change the name of your business for your Instagram account. Rather, how would you approach your Instagram name?

Let me explain why this is important. You have just 30 characters to use for your business username. Apart from that, here are a few other features of the Instagram username.

- You cannot capitalize letters in your username. This makes it challenging sometimes to distinguish two different words in your username.

- You cannot use any special characters. You may use the underscore (_) or period (.) within your username.

- You can use numbers in your username.

So let us look at a few tips to consider for creating your username.

Your Instagram Username Should Not be Different From Your Business Name

Choosing a different name for your Instagram will only seek to confuse your audience. They might wonder if the Instagram account actually belongs to your business. So always make sure that you are incorporating your business name.

Add a Keyword or Distinguishing Feature

If your business is located in New York, perhaps that would be something you should add to your username. For example, if you have a gardening business named Green Gardeners, then your username could be greengardeners.ny

Don't Use Underscores or Full Stops Excessively

Though these characters could aid you in making that original username, try to limit their usage. Overuse prevents your name from being easily picked up by search engines when people type it in the search tab. It also creates the sense that your username is a bit too complicated, which brings us to the next point: concision.

Username Length: Keeping it Concise

When it comes to having your page name easily popping up during a web search, a name that is not too long is very significant. A short and precise name makes your brand quite exclusive, as it would rank among the top results in a web search, and also prevents your potential customers from getting confused over your username. The same also goes for your full name — make it as short as possible. You do not have to use all the 30 characters of the username limit.

Leave Off Religion, Race, and Gender

This goes without saying, but do not add any religious, race, or gender affiliations in your name. If this is not the niche you are aiming for, you would be drastically restricting the possible size of your audience before you even start.

Well-Known Names

There are some names that lots of people and businesses add to their usernames to distinguish themselves from other Instagram accounts. Some of these include words such as

Entrepreneur, Success, Amazing, Top, etc. There are a host of large accounts on Instagram that have used to these usernames, and it would be very difficult to compete against them as you try to build your audience. When your customers search for your name on IG, the results bring up the most popular accounts which might not include yours since you are just beginning. Many people won't spend so much time going through the tons of names in results looking for your page. Using a distinct name will ensure it is less complicated for people to find your page when looking for you.

It Should Share Some Similarity to Your Website

Pick a username that is quite similar to your website domain name.

What this means is that if you have a web address or are planning on getting yourself a website, then make sure that your web address matches your Instagram name. Alternatively, you could also consider using an Instagram username to match your website.

Depending on the number of people that click and view your website, your position on Google search rankings could also rise. This is massive, as it means that people can easily search and find your brand even when they are not on the Instagram platform.

Have a Username That Is Secured Across All Social Media Circles

This is of major significance to individuals or brands that want to broaden their reach across all social media platforms ranging from Twitter, Snapchat, Facebook, and others. This means finding a username that you can use across all platforms. It makes your username exclusive to your brand across the platforms. There are a plethora of platforms that you can use to check if your particular username is available to you across multiple platforms. An example of such a platform is Namecheckr. Simply enter your name in the search bar, and Namecheckr will automatically show you on what platforms you can create an account with your preferred username.

Chapter 2:
How to Set Up Your Instagram Account for Maximum Effectiveness

What Kind of Content to Post?

Instagram provides you with tons of features that you can utilize for your content strategy. We had already seen how you could create a content strategy for your business. But we had simply touched the tip of the iceberg when it comes to the types of content we can create on Instagram. You are not limited to just a single image or video.

Let us look at the various content types you can bring into your strategy.

Content Type 1: Instagram Stories

Today, many businesses are routinely utilizing Instagram stories to promote their products or messages. There is a reason why this content tool is gaining popularity.

One of the main benefits of Instagram stories is that businesses can add clickable links within the stories. This means that when people watch your story, they can click-through and head over to your online store or web destination.

The best part about stories is that they disappear after a certain period of time, usually 24 hours. You can extend the duration of the stories by "highlighting" them. But the basic idea is that you can remove the stories once they have served their purpose.

Think of like setting up a billboard on a busy highway. You can keep it for 24 hours and use a new one or keep it longer for a purpose (for example, a seasonal sale, a special promotion, a competition, etc.) and then remove it.

Content Type 2: Carousel Posts

Carousel posts are simply a series of images that users can swipe through. What this means is that you can create a post that has more than one image. To move to the next image, users simply have to swipe left. This is an effective way to market your product if you have a collection of ideas or products to market.

Here is an important fact about carousel posts: after video, they are the second most engaged form of content on Instagram.

Think about that when you are laying down the groundwork for your Instagram content strategy.

Content Type 3: Live Videos

And you are live!

Live videos are all the rage these days. You can set up a date and time and start recording live while you engage with your fans!

When you want to build loyalty, it does not get any better than this.

What are some of the ways in which you can use a live video?

Idea 1: Schedule a Q&A session. Let your audience get to know you and your products better.

Idea 2: Make an announcement. When you have created a

loyal following, and you would like to introduce your customers to a new offering or product, then a live video is an exciting way to reveal your next best product or service. What's more? By creating a high level of excitement through a live session, you can create an effective word-of-mouth marketing. And we all know how potent word-of-mouth can be.

Idea 3: Behind-the-scenes action! Show them something about how you make your products. This is an effective strategy when you would like to send a little message to your audience. For example, do you create your own unique steak marinade? Then let them have a glimpse of how you create it (without revealing much about the process of course! It's your secret recipe after all).

Content Type 4: Story Polls

You can create polls within your story.

It sounds fun, doesn't it?!

Think about it this way. Let's say that you have an ice-cream store, and you enjoy creating some unique flavors every month. Why not give your audience a couple of options for the next flavor you would like them to try out and let them pick what excites them more? With just a simple question, you drive an incredible amount of engagement to your content. And you get to promote a new product at the same time.

Polls are not just limited to product introductions. You can have polls about new events, special offers, and promotions, or simply to engage with your audience about something spontaneous.

Content Type 5: Checkout

In March 2019, Instagram created waves when it mentioned a new feature called Checkout. What this feature allows users to do is to go through the product offerings of a business and instantly make purchases via Instagram. In other words, you can actually turn your Instagram into an ecommerce platform!

This new feature makes it so much easier for users to go from just browsing on the platform to buying. The transition is smooth and it doesn't interrupt the overall experience of the user. In fact, users can browse through the products knowing that they are looking through a catalog. If they are interested, then they simply have to perform a few quick "tap" commands to purchase the product.

This is another kind of post that you can utilize to direct your audience to a shopping page. In fact, you could also have two different Instagram accounts. One is used to simply market your products and other fun stuff about your awesome brand. The other account can be used as a shopping catalog, highlighting your product features. Any user who goes on the platform will clearly know why they are there. Of all the features Instagram released in 2019, this has been the favorite of many businesses and brands, for obvious reasons.

Content Type 6: Donation Stickers

Stories have grown since the time the feature was introduced on Instagram. Currently, they have over 500 million active users. They are a unique way to interact with your audience, using a combination of media, stickers, graphics, and filters to keep a certain update for a period of 24 hours before the media is removed. Of course, you can save the story that you had created and then repost it later. Understanding that stories have such a powerful influence in the minds of the people, Instagram has introduced "Donation Stickers."

What this does is that you can create a story and then add one of these stickers into it. When your audience come and notice the sticker, they can click on it and raise money for a particular cause.

How does this benefit you?

As the world evolves, so do business values. Gone are the days when businesses were only about the profit margins and revenue streams. These days, companies have to stand up for something. For that reason, if you are supporting a local charity or non-profit organization (or you are part of a non-profit organization), then you can use this feature to raise money for a particular cause.

Creating High-Quality Content

The ability to develop content that is not only of high quality but can keep your audience engaged is important if you have any plans of taking your business on Instagram to the next level. It is one thing to know what to do and another to keep the quality of your content high. Brands who are engaging with their audience on Instagram know this. They know that they should create high-quality content so they can grow. However, only very few of them end up doing this. When considering high-quality content, here are a few things you should consider:

- What is the best performing content on Instagram? What are the competitors doing? What are other brands or companies in the same business as yours doing?

- Is the content you upload on Instagram clear enough for the audience to understand?

44

There are a few things we will try and look at, which include the ways to get the right content for your account on Instagram and the factors which you should put into consideration when promoting your Instagram page with these contents.

Why Is High-Quality Instagram Content so Important?

Let's focus a bit on the Instagram algorithm. The Instagram algorithm is always subject to constant changes. Since it gets altered frequently, a lot of brands have struggled to grow.

Why is this important? When Instagram was first acquired by Facebook, getting lots of followers was easy with random posting and images of low quality. In fact, there were programs you could utilize to buy followers! Yup. Simply spend $50, and you get a program that adds about 1,000 followers to your profile. That did not seem fair to those businesses who were actually putting in the legwork to make sure they grow their audience.

A lot has changed. Consistency is now an essential aspect of growth on Instagram. You should always make posts that get the attention of your audience.

And this is what makes the Instagram algorithm unique. It is updated to seek out fake accounts and delete them. It also organizes your feed based on the engagement that posts receive, with the most engaged posts showing up on top of your feed, followed by posts having lesser engagement.

This means that as soon as the Instagram algorithm notices that your audience is engaged with your post, it automatically gives your post greater visibility on the platform.

The ability to make create good content for your Instagram

account will do much more than help you grow your account. It can put you in the eye of big firms. A lot of firms are interested in partnering with businesses to help create good content for their Instagram account and website. This means that if you can create an impact on the platform with your content, a big firm might be willing to work with you.

Planning Your Instagram Content

There are two vital questions to answer before going ahead with the Instagram content planning. These questions are:

- What content is most suitable for your brand?

- What kind of content is your audience interested in?

Successfully deciphering the why, what and who concerning your Instagram brand is a step you should take when getting your content planned. The knowledge of what your audience expects and the details about your brand will come in handy in assisting you in developing the right content from the outset.

You will make a lot of progress by discovering what niche your brand is and putting in all your focus on just that niche. The level of growth that a lot of accounts on Instagram expect does not come forth because of a lack of focus.

This means that if you are a business that is about food, most of the content you develop has to be about food. You can stray a little when you feel like you would like to cover a trending topic. But ideally, you have to make sure that you stick to your niche so that you satisfy your audience's expectations.

As soon as you successfully provide answers to the two questions above, the next thing to do is get your content for the week planned out.

To get started, you should have a list of the content that you have planned to put on your page for a week. This could be more than a week if you think that is convenient for you. While making a list, ensure that there is a variety. With variety, you can be confident that your audience will not be bored even though you are focused on your niche. Need help creating unique content? Use the tips I provided to develop a content strategy along with the list of unique content available to you.

Additionally, plan ahead in advance. For example, if you are planning to have a collection of images of your products, then a tried and trusted way to achieve so much from a short time is to carry out photoshoots for content that will cover an extended period at once.

If you can consistently get content for an extended period ready in just one week, you will be able to save yourself some time, as you will always have content for the weeks ahead.

The quality of content you post on Instagram will be higher as you get better organized.

Take Advantage of Ready-to-Use Templates

Another thing that you can do - especially when you are posting images - is that you can use the many tools that can be of help to you. Some of these tools are Canva, Venngage, and Spark Post. These tools will go a long way in helping you develop great visuals for Instagram.

It does not matter what you want to achieve. Do you want to promote a recipe you already posted on your blog? Do you want to craft a post that can help in bringing a special offer to the limelight?

You can explore a host of ideas through the various platforms available to you.

Shooting Your Instagram Content Photos

When you are aiming to create your own photos, then one of your hurdles might just be the choice of the camera that you would like to use. Regarding this, you do not have to get the best camera in town.

You can create some incredible content just by the use of a quality phone camera.

In as much as you can get outstanding quality images with the use of a high-quality camera, there are factors which can significantly influence the success of your Instagram account. These factors include the composition as well as the content of your photos. You have no cause to worry if you cannot afford the best camera in town. What you need to focus on is having a good plan for the outcome of your photos.

Some of the things that you should consider while planning your photos are the camera angle, composition, and lighting.

Here are a few tips that you can practice.

Tip #1

Always ensure that you snap more pictures than you need. This will give you a wider range of pictures to select from.

Tip #2

When taking lots of pictures, you should alter the appearance of the various photos by altering the pose, your camera angle, the distance between your product and the camera, and much more. These changes might seem insignificant, but they will go a long way in ensuring that you have a wider array of choices available to you.

Tip #3

Always make sure you keep a few of the original images untouched by visual editing. This allows you to easily fall back to a photo if you do not like the changes you have applied.

Tip #4

Use different devices, if possible. This allows you to gauge the quality of the pictures you are taking.

By following the tips above, you will be able to select the best pictures for your account. However, besides having options for pictures, you also have content that can come in handy in case you fail to create content in the future.

Let's take an example. If you are a food blogger and you just discovered a lip-smacking steak smothered in an incredibly sweet and spicy BBQ sauce (boy, that sounds rather tempting right now), you might decide to make your audience aware of the food you discovered by posting pictures of them. There is a likelihood that in the coming weeks, you might want to remind your audience of that food or you might just not be in a position to capture more content. When you already have a number of content, then you won't have to worry. You have already taken various pictures from just one shoot.

Find High-Quality Stock Images

In very recent times, stock images have been viewed in a negative light. This is because content creators think that there is no effort put into creating content when stock images are used. It's simply a matter of taking a stock image, adding a little text and voila! You are done.

However, if you look at the workings of marketing agencies

around the world, then you should realize that they use stock images heavily (so don't worry about using them for your content).

Regardless of what feedback they receive, you can still get the best out of them.

Stock images can go a long way in helping you develop a feed that is varied when they are used alongside other images. It is still important to keep in mind that although stock images can be beneficial, not all of them should be given so much attention as they are sometimes of low quality.

If you are not sure how to get good quality images that are not so "stocky," go to websites such as Stocksnap.io. or Unsplash. At these sites, you can get images that are ideal for what you do and, amazingly, they are free.

If you are ready to spend some money on getting suitable pictures, Stocksy will be a good site for you. You can get images of higher quality and also have a broader range to choose from.

To get the best out of Instagram posts, you should post pictures with dimensions 1080p x 1080p.

Aim for High-Content Across All Your Content

If you are creating a video, then make sure that you have the right device to use for the purpose. If you are shooting a live video, then ensure that your audience can see you clearly. No matter what content you create, you should focus on the following:

- Visual Clarity: People do not like to spend time on a video that is not clear or makes it difficult for them to see.

- Length of the Content: Can you achieve to send across your message in a few seconds rather than a few minutes? Then you should do so!

- Audio Clarity: Equally important to the visual quality of a video is the audio quality. You cannot have someone watching a video and barely understand a word you are saying.

Use a Dummy Account for Practice

If you are unsure about how well your image or video (or live stream) looks, then you can create a dummy account and try out your content before you officially publish. Make sure that your dummy account is set to private. You do not want your audience discovering your content on another account.

Posting Your Instagram Content

The posting comes right after planning your content, creating them, and making sure your content is of high quality.

Posting is way beyond putting up images on your account. Strategic planning is important. When posted strategically, your posts can help grow your account very rapidly.

When getting ready to post, always ensure that you do not post similar photos side by side. In fact, do not even post similar types of content close to one another. Keep at least a two-week gap between posts. The simple reason is posting similar photos close to one another can make your audience feel bored, as they do not see a variety from your end.

There are lots of ways to plan your post. You can either do it by uploading them directly to Instagram or using external programs such as Later's Visual Planner. With Later's Visual

Planner, you will be able to see a glimpse of the posts you have planned the way they would appear before they finally get posted. This, therefore, gives you the privilege to make vital changes before making a post.

As soon as you get satisfied with the appearance of your posts, you can go ahead and schedule your posts.

While a lot of people stop at posting, that is not where the work ends. One way to grow your Instagram account is to engage your audience. It is crucial that you respond to each comment you get. When people comment on your posts, you can engage with them by liking their posts.

When you do this, it is beneficial in a couple of ways. It makes the Instagram algorithm understand that you and your followers have a relationship. As a result of this, your content can appear higher in their feeds.

Also, relating to your followers helps you know them better and build a stronger relationship with them. This is perfect because it is one primary reason for the existence of Instagram.

If you give attention to your audience and niche and put in a lot of effort into the planning, the shooting, the editing, and the posting of content, you will experience steady growth.

Don't Worry About Likes

Instagram has recently launched an update that removes "likes" from the platform. Now, just to be precise, you can still see that people have liked your post, but you are not able to see the number of likes on the post anymore.

If you have a business account, you can use the analytics section to look at details of the likes and other components that make up your post to see how well your content is doing on the platform. However, you won't be able to directly see the number of likes on the content and neither will your audience be privy to such information.

Instagram feels that people should focus more on the quality of content rather than focusing on "likes." And, this is an important business strategy for you to consider, as well.

Sometimes, people see the number of likes and instantly form opinions on posts. That means, if you are a new business and you are creating quality content, then people might notice the number of likes your post has and automatically make judgments about your content. If you have a low number of likes, despite your content being well thought out and creative, the audience might just skip to another piece of content that has more likes. This gives an unfair advantage to bigger organizations and people with large followers. By hiding the number of likes, Instagram is evening out the playing field, giving equal opportunities to all businesses.

This means that when people come to your business or brand's account, they will be able to judge your content based on its quality, and not because of the number of likes you've collected. Which is why you should focus, primarily, on creating quality content.

Other Ways to Get Quality Content

There are ways you can get content beyond developing your own content. Let us take a look at some of the most trusted methods below.

Run a UGC Campaign

When trying to find content that was not created by you, you do not have to depend solely on your own content. You can also get your followers to develop content with a topic in focus.

When you obtain content this way, it is called a "UGC." UGC stands for user-generated content. This term can be used for any content that users of a product created for that product.

To get your followers to create posts for you, one thing you should do is create a competition in which the winner gets a price. Simply get your audience to take pictures or videos of your product, venue, or service, and you could reward them with some cool prices.

Alternatively, you can start using a unique hashtag in your posts. So, let's say that you have a sports equipment business named Active McSporty (not the most imaginative name, but let's run with it). Soy our hashtags should be something like.

- #ActiveMcSporty

- #ActiveMcS

- #ActiveMcSportyNY (if you are located in New York)

Why do you have to create unique hashtags? If you have a hashtag that is already in use, then you are sharing your content space with other people. This means that your hashtag will get flooded with content from people who are not supporting your business but are simply using the hashtag for promoting their own posts.

However, it is vital that you do not depend on user-generated content for getting the majority of your content. Your audience might feel exploited if you always take advantage of them.

Collaborate With Influencers

Collaborating with influencers is a trusted way to have a constant supply of on-brand content on Instagram. Partnering with influencers can help you reach more people. The simple reason for this is influencers have a sizeable number of followers already.

The flip side to this is that influencers can be quite pricey. As a result of this, if you are running on a low budget, you might decide to work with micro-influencers before going on to work with more established influencers.

By working with micro-influencers, you can reach between 10,000 to 50,000 people. This is very efficient if you work with influencers in your niche.

To get in touch with influencers, send them a message on Instagram. However, sending a message is not essential as you can get their contact details from their bios.

Add Call-to-Action in Your Posts

Don't just share pictures and content with your audience. Try to get them to take an action. You could direct them to your website or you could encourage them to purchase a product. Alternatively, you could even inform them to follow your Instagram account. These messages to encourage the audience to take a particular action are known as "call-to-actions." With that said, you don't have to keep telling your audience to do something in each post. They might get pretty annoyed with that tactic. But add in call-to-actions as frequently as possible, without spamming the feeds of your audience.

You don't have to directly use a call-to-action post. There are ways to indirectly encourage your audience to take action. For example, talk about your product features and include a link to your website or online store, a phone number for the audience to get in touch with you, or the address of your physical store. That way, you don't have to always notify your audience to do something. They will enjoy the content that you post on the platform, but they are also given the option of taking an action through subtle and clever placements of various links and contact options.

Create a Diverse Content

Don't stick to one type of content. Look at what people are doing out there and incorporate different ideas into your posts. What is the latest trend? What kind of posts do people prefer more?

At the same time, don't just focus on photos. People love novelty. When you combine different kinds of media, you are keeping your content fresh and exciting.

Let us look at this point using a content calendar.

Day	Type of Post
Sunday	Photo
Monday	Photo
Tuesday	Photo
Wednesday	Photo
Thursday	Video

You already know that people can easily change their opinion about your content. You don't have to necessarily wait for a week or so to see people's interest in your posts. Which is why, if you look at the above content schedule, then your audience interest might drop by Tuesday or Wednesday. By Thursday, you will barely have an audience to watch that exciting video that you were planning to put up. Sure, you might not have videos to put up each and every day. But you still need to show your audience that you are more than just a photo album.

Look at the content schedule below.

Day	Type of Post
Sunday	Photo
Monday	Photo
Tuesday	Video
Wednesday	Photo
Thursday	Photo

Notice the difference? You haven't done anything new. You have simply moved the video content to Tuesday. Your audience realizes that you have some cool exciting videos to show as well. You can then choose to show photos for some days before adding another video. Because, by that point, your audience already knows that you are capable of creating unique content. They don't mind waiting for it.

Think Saves

What would make people save your posts? How exciting can you make it in order for people to actually add it to their collection of posts?

Think in terms of longevity. But why saves? Isn't it enough for people to come and see your post and leave a comment?

Not anymore.

In 2019, Instagram improved its algorithm so that even saves are counted as important engagement. So, what does "important engagement" actually mean? Here's the gist of it. Any content that is important for the engagement of the platform is given priority. Instagram arranges posts on your feed based on their importance and value. And how does Instagram judge the value of a content?

The platform leaves it to the audience to decide. When the audience give a like or leaves a comment, Instagram improves the value of the post. Instagram knows that visitors don't usually save a post. Which is why saving adds slightly more value to the post than other forms of engagement.

Think in terms of saves, then. How creative can you make your post? How engaging can they be? What message would you like to communicate with your audience? Think about how you can even use the opportunity to promote your products or yourself.

Create a Story For Your Feed Post

Here is a neat little trick that you can use on Instagram that most people won't tell you. When you create a particular post on Instagram, then upload the same post into your story! Instagram stories improve the visibility of your content by a huge margin, so why not use it to your advantage, and as much as possible?

How quickly you would like to upload content to the story is entirely up to you. You could wait for a couple of hours before using the post in your story. But I like to believe that you should create a strategy based on your post.

Let's take an example. If you have a post that is bringing in more engagement, then pushing out a story about that post will not allow you to make use of the full potential of stories. So, what should you do in such a scenario? First, let the post accumulate more and more engagement. In fact, you can wait for an entire day to pass. After about 24 hours, you can launch an Instagram story about that post, boosting your post's engagement even more!

On the other hand, let's assume that you have a post that is raking in poor engagement. Then you don't have to wait for 24 hours to launch it in story format. Boost its engagement by posting a story about it within a couple or few hours.

Such tactics allow you to adjust the engagement of your content to your liking. Which is why it is important to keep an eye out on your analytics. Check the numbers and progress each post makes. Use informed decisions to guide your content. Try not to take action on an impulse. Make sure you get as much information as possible about your idea.

Outsourcing Posting and Programs Available to Schedule Posting

There is a range of tools you can use for scheduling posting. Below are some of your top options:

Later Application

This application creates a direct link for scheduling and publishing your various social media application, such as Pinterest, Facebook, Twitter, and Instagram. This application enables you to copy pictures from your mobile or desktop devices to an online scheduling service called Later Calendar, giving you the opportunity to upload them at the indicated time. The app readily compliments your schedule because you can use it to post your content at a time that is convenient for you. Note that if you create your Later App with Instagram, you will receive an instruction directing you to configure direct publishing. What this means is that you are giving the app permission to publish directly on Instagram.

Sendible

Unlike Later Application, Sendible is not free. It offers various services on more than three social platforms, such as following the hashtag trends on Twitter or posting directly to Instagram and Facebook. You can purchase a plan from $30 per month. The major advantage of Sendible is its ability to upload various posts on more than one social media platform simultaneously. This becomes important when you are managing multiple social media platforms.

Hootsuite

Hootsuite serves as a great advantage to every social media user, be it for your personal use, for your business, or even for professional use. It has different plans specified for your needs. These plans include a free plan, business plan, and professional plan. Each plan has unique features. The free plan is restricted to schedule no more than 29 messages across only three social media platform. To upgrade, you would need to purchase a business plan, which is $30. This plan is unlimited and gives you the ability to schedule within 10 different social media platforms. One unique feature of Hootsuite is that you can schedule to upload a post at a convenient time.

Zoho Social

Like the above-mentioned applications, Zoho Social presents a direct link for uploading or publishing on any social media platform. This includes the likes of Instagram, Facebook, Instagram, Twitter, and LinkedIn. Zoho Social can only be directly published to any of your specified social networks when you grant your permission. Once this is done, there is a direct link between your account and your social media profile. The application comes in a free version and a paid version, which costs $10 per month. The former has special features to the advantage of the user and can be used by more than one person.

Postcron

You can download a Postcron application for the sum of $15 and above for a month. This plan helps you manage more than nine social media accounts and also schedules 200 posts every month. To test run the application, it offers you a week free trial, after which you will have to choose a payment plan. Postcron can be directly linked through different social media platforms, including Facebook, LinkedIn, and Twitter. If your Postcron account is directly linked to your Instagram account, you can upload more than one post at a time.

Sprout Social

The primary advantage of Sprout Social is that it presents the opportunity to upload, post, and schedule all at the same time. This type of application is best utilized by marketers. It grants access to more than two team members to make contributions to the agreed schedule. The team members can separately supervise the progress of what is being posted and uploaded.

Chapter 3:
Most Common Methods Used to Make Your Profile Attractive and Effective

There is a reason why Instagram is rated among the most effective means by which established and upcoming brands make their presence felt in the social media space.

This is because you devote a lot of time and commitment towards building an identity for your brand on Instagram, which you can only attain by critically thinking of a pattern to follow and by sticking to it. You take the time to create a brand identity and manage it. But unlike other platforms, Instagram shows you results.

Why? Because Instagram is a visual medium, and you are using visuals to convey your message.

Now you might be confused. You might ask me; is that all author? That's the main reason?

Well, think of it this way: Facebook is a visual and text medium. People upload images, push on status messages, and so on. Twitter is similar, as well. Now, that does not mean that Instagram is not a visual and text medium. But its main focus is visuals, which is why you are using its main focus to build your brand. You are bound to get feedback and responses based on the efforts you put into it.

Which is why you need to have a plan of action when you are working on your Instagram's visual identity (a.k.a. content strategy). When you randomly put up posts about anything, you tend to lose followers because these random posts do not have anything to do with your brand.

The Benefits of Consistent Branding

A properly designed and consistent branding is crucial for your business. If you have consistent Instagram posts, the following are some of the benefits you stand to gain.

They Include:

- Precise first impression: Having a well-planned out and consistent design gives first-time visitors to your page a pretty good idea what your brand is all about.

- Trustworthiness: You garner a lot of trust from people online when the content of your posts is tailored towards your brand as opposed to posting anything random.

- Distinction: When you are consistent with your postings, it distinguishes you from your competitors. However, inconsistency does the opposite. It makes you no different from the tons of accounts out there.

- Brand identity: Make sure your posts are well thought out and go with your designs aesthetic so that people online have a precise idea of what your brand personality is all about.

- Easy To Recognize: By being consistent with your postings, it will be easy for customers to recognize your brand.

Having learned how you can brand your business and the benefits you can reap off the process, the next step to learn is how to create a cohesive brand on Instagram.

So how do you do this? Let us find out below.

How to Create a Cohesive Instagram Brand
Work Out Your Brand Personality

Your goal is to have consistent Instagram content. For this reason, it is ideal for you to determine the identity of your brand.

As stated by Business 2 Community, the following are a few factors you should consider:

- **Know The Type of People Who Will Use Your Product**: Determining the class and age range of the people who would primarily make use of your branded products is vital. When you do this, consider how they would use the products or services you are offering.

- **Carry Out Statistical Research**: Check out successful Instagram influencers online who are in a similar niche as yours or trying to sell to a similar audience. Look at their postings and check out their statistics. You can go a step further and take a look at what their competitors are doing. Their strategies should aid you in coining out a strategy for yourself.

- **Decide the Audio and Visual Content to Share**: Analyze your target audience. Would they want funny, educational, or informational content? For the best results, you need to plan this strategically.

- **Add a Bit of Creativity**: Creativity is essential. Do not ignore captions. You need to incorporate informative or fun posts with your visual content. Hashtags are also essential, and you should not forget them. As stated by a recent study, posts that had 11 hashtags or above got almost 80% engagement. This is as opposed to just 22% when utilizing 10 hashtags.

Pick a Theme (Visuals)

Next, you need to pick a theme. Themes have to do with a niche or subject matter. It could also consist of your page patterns and compositions. Essentially, you are choosing the way your page is set up.

A theme will aid you in connecting with your audiences, pointing out your niche, developing your follower's base, and identifying essential hashtags.

If you are in Instagram for business, all you need to do is to pick a theme that goes with your business, similar to what most large brands do. If this is not the case, all you have to do is to choose a theme that triggers some excitement in you and go with it.

When picking a theme, the following are ideas to consider:

- White

- Vintage

- Beige

- Colorful

If you are not satisfied with your account theme, you can always change it later until you get what fits.

Now, what exactly do I mean by a theme? Think of a theme as your color palette. If you have a clothing store, then your theme is mostly going to be a white background. That is because you do not want anything distracting the viewer's eye from the object of their focus (your collection of clothing and apparel).

If it is food, then perhaps your theme could be a brown wooden table (especially if you want to give an all-natural feel to your visuals).

In such ways, you need to decide how you can best attract your audience. Now, remember one thing, you do not always have to stick to your theme. Some of your visuals can deviate from the theme whenever you feel that they should. However, your theme dictates your overall approach to your images.

Get Inspiration From Other Pages on Instagram

If you are unable to find something that suits you, then an easier way is to check out other pages on Instagram for inspiration. However, ensure these pages are in the same niche as yours.

If you find these pages appealing to your aesthetic taste, become a follower of such pages. Then ask yourself these questions:

- Are these pages among my brand niche? What attracts me to these pages?

- Do I feel inspired when I look at these pages? Do these pages motivate me?

- What particular aesthetic design fits my brand?

Observing the aesthetic details on these explored pages could inspire you as to how you should go about designing your page in a way that showcases the identity of your brand.

Have an Aesthetic Reference Guide

Huge firms have a style reference guide through which they can maintain an aesthetic appearance that is consistent with their Instagram pages.

These guides usually consist of the filters, colors, and kinds of aesthetic and content they will utilize. This makes sure that any of their team members will have a guideline or reference to follow when they are creating posts on the page.

The reference guides should not be complicated and should be easy for any member of your social media marketing team to refer to.

Craft a Story

Having a good storyline that tells followers what your brand stands for is a good way of making a hit on Instagram with your page. The story makes your followers connect with your brand as they can relate with it on an emotional level. It also gives valuable meaning to the content of your posts.

Kick Off Your Design

Once you have finalized your visual design, it is time to create it. You could develop your pictures by yourself or work alongside a team; it is entirely up to you.

You need to develop ideas for photo shoots, plan the kinds of posts, the location you would take photos and other essentials that you will add for every post. You can pen drafts of posts or look at similar photos on Instagram to give you an idea of its feel and look.

A great tip is to place yourself in the viewer's perspective;

- In what way does your composition stand out?

- What would your followers feel when they look at your images? If they were going through your feed, would it draw them in?

- When do you start shooting videos or photos? What location would be ideal?

- Which particular photo lighting gadgets would make for a great photoshoot or video shoot?

- How about images that use graphics? How do they fit into your narrative and overall theme?

- If you are creating animations, what can you do to make sure that your end result is sticking to your theme?

Get Your Story Right

Finally, creating a brand identity is not just about having the right visuals.

It is about your story. It is about your messaging.

What are you trying to be?

- Are you aiming to be adventurous like Red Bull or GoPro?

- Are you thinking of being informative like NASA or National Geographic?

- Are you hoping to be humanitarian or emotional like the Red Cross society?

Your story and messaging are important. Without it, you might start having a particular personality at one point and another one at a different point. People might not just be confused about what you are trying to convey but wonder if your brand is going through some drastic changes.

At its core, your story isn't actually about your company. Your company is the physical embodiment of your story, but the purpose of your story is to establish a connection with your customers.

You should tell your story in such a manner that it lets your customers know that you can relate to them, that you understand them, and you care about their interests.

Nike is focused on athletes and people interested in sports. Their content encourages an active lifestyle, and they make sure that the models used in their visuals are people from various race, gender, and ethnic background. This shows that their products cater to anyone in the world.

That is Nike messaging.

What is yours?

What are you trying to say?

How can you connect with your customers through a story?

Few ideas of marketing can communicate the level of engagement a story can.

Filters and Photo Software to Use

If you plan on creating an Instagram feed that is cohesive, there has to be consistency in your editing process. You need to select the same fonts, filters, and options when editing.

There are numerous editing tools you can take advantage of on Instagram. If you are not satisfied with their options, you can take a look at other applications like:

Adobe Photoshop (Lightroom Edition)

The Adobe collection of software for photography has made a name for itself over the years. It is perhaps one of the best in the photography market scene. For lots of professional photographers, it is an indispensable tool.

The tools are perhaps ideal for individuals who are genuinely passionate about photography and desire an editing application that offers in-depth editing features on the move. This solution offers users a lighter version of what the desktop app offers. It gives you the capacity to change standard mobile images into amazing versions.

Are you a fan of tools? Then this is not a problem, as it comes with a barrage of them which let you tweak almost all aspect of an image. There are also preset filters which you can utilize with ease.

The application also comes alongside an in-built camera. You can equally go a step further with the pro mode, as it offers you authority over settings like ISO, Shutter Speed, and White Balance.

This application is ideal for individuals who are serious about photography. It is also great for those who want to step up their

Instagram picture quality. If you want to find out more about editing pictures, you are not left out. Just by checking out all aspects of the application, you are sure to learn something new that will help improve your photo editing skills.

VSCO Photo Application

This application for editing photos is well-recognized by numerous Instagram users. The application goes beyond editing photos. It provides a community where photographers are able to create and make connections, which becomes essential when you would like to exchange ideas with other professionals from around the world.

The application comes alongside tools you can expect to find in a great app for editing photos. Some of these include highlights, saturation, vignette, and temperature. The great part is that it gives you control over all of these and many other settings.

VSCO also comes alongside an in-built camera with comprehensive control. With it, you will be able to take a shot, edit it, and save it. You can do all of these from the application itself. In terms of convenience, this is a very fantastic option.

VSCO also focuses on its filters as you can purchase filter packs. All of these packs come with their unique tones and styles and are well-known among individuals who utilize the application. The application also provides a distinct user experience alongside a fantastic interface.

If you are someone who wants to take his Instagram to the next phase, this is undoubtedly an application to take advantage of.

Prisma

Prisma is one of the latest photo editing apps with great

prospects, and it is becoming popular among users. The app is quite easy to utilize and may be addictive. The app <u>Prisma</u> works by turning a standard photo into great artistic work through filtering. However, these are not the usual Valencia and Lo-fi filters.

The Artistic Modern Filters, which are preloaded on the Prisma app, mimic the great works of famous painters as Picasso and van Gogh and even that of the famous Mondrian. An image can be completely made over to spice up your updates on Instagram.

And recently, the developers of the app added a social feature which gives the users the medium to connect with their friends. The app currently boasts of about 40 filters, and this number is likely to increase judging from the success the app has enjoyed.

Prisma is free, cool, and filled with so much fun, and your content is poised to have an excellent artistic makeover.

Afterlight

This app is not only simple to use, but it also offers quality filters and excellent functions. All of these works together to offer you a wonderful user experience. However, it requires payment to take advantage of what it has to offer.

The <u>Afterlight </u> app is a standard app, and it boasts of all the editing tools that you might expect to see in an app of that caliber: The saturation, exposure, contrast, as well as the RBG Shadow tones, are all adjustable. This is not all, as there is a lot more to enjoy with the app.

Afterlight is simply one of the best apps in the area of filtering, and it boasts tons of filters that will give you the best experience. There are more filters available here than Instagram has to offer, so it would make a great choice if you want more filters.

In Afterlight, you have the opportunity to stack filters. You can also enhance your photos with frames. You will also be able to send out your photos in HD resolution.

One of the best features of the app is textured filters, especially the light leak. This filter boasts of excellent quality, and if used on a standard photo, will make the light flares seem natural.

All the effects and filters in the app can be adjusted, so you have absolute control over the form in which your photo comes out.

If you are looking for that photo that stands out from others, then the $0.99 cost of the app is worth paying for.

Others include:

- A Color Story

- Camera+

- Pro-Camera

How to Take High-Quality Photos

By now, you understand that improving your game when it comes to photos you upload on your Instagram helps you boost your brand presence on the platform.

Your next approach is to figure out just how you are going to get these high-quality photos. So, let us get right down to it.

How to Take Great Instagram Photos

Now that you understand how crucial it is to step up your game when it comes to photography, you may begin to imagine your next step. How exactly can you enhance your photo quality the right way? Is there a way to do it quickly? How are you going to go from creating photos that seem like they could be taken by anyone to creating pieces of art that look like they belong in a museum?

Below, we will be taking a look at a few tips that can help you move from creating ordinary Instagram photos to awesome Instagram photos. Now, let us take a look at what these steps are.

Plan Your Aesthetic

Instagram has a very basic design that is easily identifiable; it is designed in such a way that the photos you upload will appear once on your followers' timelines. But the moment they click on your profile, they can see all the photos that you have been collectively uploaded.

You need to look at your Instagram page from an outsider's perspective. What do you think about the arrangement of photos? Do you like the way you organize your visuals? Try and get someone else's assistant. See what they think of your Instagram's photo arrangement.

With that in mind, you need to imagine how you want your Instagram design to look like as a whole. You need to do this even before you take another picture.

Also, remember that the entire Instagram aesthetic of your page should complement what your brand stands for. There should not be a deviation from the identity you have created on the minds of your audience.

Think of what you are going to capture. How many subjects are going to be present in your image? Would you require numerous landscape shots because you need a wide angle to capture a lot of visual information? Do you need a portrait shot? Other things to think about are the settings. For example, you have a showroom, and perhaps your feed would be about cars; would they be best in a showroom or outdoors?

Having a plan ahead will assist you in taking great Instagram photos as well as photos that add more to your brand identity. The next thing after your shots are taken is to start planning on how to turn them into fantastic Instagram grids.

Take Time to Prepare

The fact is, taking great Instagram photos on the go would not be possible without the right amount of help from lady luck. Which is why it is always important to plan ahead.

What exactly should you consider in order to lay down the plans for your work? Let's look at a few questions:

- Is it necessary to buy props to include in your photos?

- Is there a need for you to go to other locations, which will make your photos more appealing?

- Will you need other supplies, such as a backdrop, especially for photos that will be laid on flat surfaces?

- Do you plan on adding other individuals in your photos? Do you have to get models who would love to be a part of it?

If your answer is yes, then you might need to take your time to put everything in order.

This way, you will be fully prepared to snap the best photos without wasting your time any further.

Understand Your Tools

Do you believe it is essential to invest in high-level lighting and cameras for your visuals? If yes, you need to reconsider. You may be amazed to know that the majority of the fantastic photos that you have come across on Instagram were taken with a mobile phone camera.

However, even if you are not spending much on gadgets, what matters more is that you understand how you can leverage on your available resources, even if it is a phone.

Just because a phone has a user-friendly camera doesn't mean that it does not come with great options. There is a barrage of options which you can take advantage of to adjust focus and exposure while utilizing a phone camera. Do note that this is dependent on the kind of phone that you have at your disposal.

This does not mean you should completely avoid using high-end equipment. If you have the ability to get yourself some advanced tools, then perhaps you should.

Below are a few DSLR cameras that you can consider for your next Instagram photoshoot:

- Sony α7 III

- Canon T6i

- Canon 5D Mark IV

Each of the cameras mentioned above has their own price and features, so go ahead and pick the one that is right for you.

Understand the Basics of Photography

You do not need to be a professional to create amazing pictures. However, there is a limit to how far those few tricks and tweaks you know can get you when it comes to taking amazing pictures.

If you plan on capturing distinct Instagram photos, it is ideal to familiarize yourself with some fundamentals of photography. It will aid you in initially getting amazing photos, which you can then transform to more amazing photos after polishing up before you post.

Photography is quite complex, and we certainly cannot cover everything about it. However, there are few things that you can look out for when taking a shot:

- **Composition**: This is the way you arrange the subject of your photo. The easiest tip for starters to have a balanced image is to utilize the <u>rule of thirds</u>.

- **Negative Space**: This is that area which encompasses that major point of interest in your photo. Adequate negative space will aid in drawing the eyes of viewers towards the most crucial element without excess clutter.

- **Perspective**: Taking a picture of your subject matter straight on is the most common method. However, to have interesting images, you can try to capture your subject from varying angles — it could be from the right or left, below or above.

- **Lighting**: It is essential that your photos have adequate light to create a perfect Instagram photo (we will be taking a more detailed look at this below).

Another critical lesson is: If it is helpful, take your pictures in the "square" mode.

So, what exactly is the square mode?

When you take a picture, you might notice one thing about the finished image; its dimensions. Sometimes, your images look like a rectangle extending horizontally (these are your typical landscape images). At other times, they might look like a rectangle extending vertically (these are your portrait images). However, some photos might have a square dimension.

Those are the types of photos that you should be aiming to capture.

This is because the majority of the images on Instagram are square. So, when you shoot in that manner, you will be able to view the exact way its structure will be. This is better than you becoming upset when you take an image with different dimensions and then end up having to crop the picture.

If your goal is to learn about the numerous techniques in photography comprehensively, it is best to get all the tutorials, classes, and even articles available at your disposal!

But if this is not the case, it is best to understand the basics of what it takes to make a great photo. Doing that alone will make a lot of difference.

Work on Your Lighting

You need to pay attention to lighting if you want to create noticeably great images. This does not imply that you have to purchase the latest lighting equipment you can find. You can make use of natural lighting, provided by our good old friend, the sun.

Also, this does not imply you need to wait for the sun to be shining bright to take advantage of natural light. No, far from it. Working with direct sunlight can be very difficult as a result of the numerous glares and shadows it casts.

So, if you have plans to take shots outdoors, you need to search for various locations with open shade. This way, you will be able to leverage natural lighting without having to deal with the problems direct sunlight brings with it.

For instance, you could place your topic of interest close to a window. But you need to note that it could be a bad idea taking shots in front of your light source directly. This is because it tends to create a shadow. A better option would be to open up your blinds so the light can come into the room and enhance the way your pictures look immediately.

Irrespective of the route you choose to take, note that even a little level of natural light can be of great benefit when it has to do with Instagram images.

One of the best times to make use of natural lighting is during a couple of hours after sunrise and a couple of hours before sunset.

Don't Rush It

Slow and steady wins the race. In this case, slow and careful planning, along with steady hands makes your Instagram look awesome.

Because Instagram is a visual platform, you may want to upload lots of pictures in quick succession. This is a mistake.

One of the ideal methods of capturing amazing images for your brand is not to rush it. This is the case, especially when taking shots yourself.

When taking shots in quick succession on your camera, take a little break, and check out the images. Ask yourself these questions:

- What do you love about them?

- What don't you fancy?

- What areas can you make changes?

Next, make a little change. These could range from the background, pose, angle, or any other aspect. This may not be applicable in all circumstances but do it when you can.

If you can invest the time, ensure you do not rush images. You can make changes while taking shots; it will ensure you have a higher possibility of getting a pleasing image. What is more, you will have a range of images that are different as opposed to those that look the same. This form of diversity will ensure that when you do make a choice, you will end up with the best of them all.

Perfection Comes Through Practice

It's not only about Instagram. Lots of things in life cannot just pan out within seconds. And it's clear that many of us want things to happen miraculously and in our way, too. We want the immediate best outcome at the first trial. So, as with anything in life, to get the best for your Instagram photo, you have to practice over and over again. And you can be sure that within a short period, you will begin to generate incredible results, and your photos start getting the best look you want for them.

Getting a great picture will only come through trying and

experimenting. But that does not mean you won't make mistakes even if you have professionals guiding you. Never give up or be frustrated as a result of the inability to get the desired result at first try. Rome, we are told, was not built in a day. It took years to give rise to a great city. Fortunately for you, you won't have to take years to get one picture right.

If you don't like a result, continue to edit; continue to practice; continue again and again. And after several attempts, you'll find out what your likes and dislikes are in photo editing. It's that simple. Even in the process of failure, you're aware of what features works well and which don't for your result.

Understand The Culture

In today's world, people are becoming more aware of the concept of human dignity and respect. One of the things that you should remember is that when creating content, you should take into consideration the culture, practices, and habits of the local population. This prevents you from creating any content that might hurt the sentiment of the local population.

We are also entering into an age of representation. This means that regardless of your ethnicity, gender, or culture, you are represented equally. Do not create any content that might offend a particular group of people. Focus on being neutral. It is understandable that you have political and social views of your own. You are human with certain belief systems. But do not merge your opinions with your business promotions. Keep both things separate. Make sure that you keep your advertisements clean. Respect the local customs.

Chapter 4:
What to Post for Best Results

People often ask why their posts on Instagram don't get the desired attention, likes, comments, or shares that they want them to. The short answer? They have not mastered the art of time. It is not so much about the urge to post content on Instagram. It is not just about getting 24/7 availability and presence on Instagram. It is much more about the incredibility of the post; it is more about timing; it has more to do with knowing where the interest of the target audience lies; it is more about who the post targets and what you want to achieve with it.

Finding the best time to get your audience to respond to your Instagram post by way of like, comment or share requires that you are aware and pragmatic. You've got to know when your audience is active to be engaged on the Instagram platform. Once you can spot this, be sure that you can post a little ahead of their active timings and your community will get the best engagement from your posts.

Here is what you need to find out about Instagram continually: once you can spot the peak hour as well as the off periods of your community, you'll stop posting content that won't get any engagement. And once you're able to engage your audience and community members meaningfully on Instagram, and they respond quickly to your posts by sharing, liking or commenting; you show a significant increase in engagement and the platform notices that and notes that you often share quality content to your feeds. It becomes a win-win for all parties: Instagram, you and your community. The rule of thumb is that you find out what time works for your community and what time doesn't. But again, that will require time, patience, and numerous tries until you get the right fit.

Is Timing Really Crucial?

Like we have earlier said, time and patience are the key factors you should adopt into your strategy.

Never undermine the power of timing. It matters. It is vital for your growth on Instagram. When your posts don't get responses, it only suggests one thing: you're churning out quantitative content that lacks quality. And that brings down your rating. So, let it be emphasized that timing matters.

Besides timing, there are other key factors you need to watch out for to be able to get a quick response and engage your community actively. While the timing and quick response to posts no doubt matter because Instagram has now shifted attention to the relevance-based algorithm and prefers that over and above the chronology (that is timeline) of the post, knowing these other factors will make you understand whether users see your post on time. What this means is that if the audience engages with your post, then that matters more to Instagram than how many posts you push out during the day.

So, talking in terms of old and recent posts on feeds, these crucial factors that Instagram uses to make users see your engagement on the platform should be taken seriously.

Here are some crucial factors that will determine if your content gets priority on Instagram or not. It also shows whether or not your followers can see your post as soon as they should so they can respond and get engaged. We will come back to the benefits of posting shortly.

Consider relevance, relationship, and recent. Does that make any sense to you?

- **Relevance:** Instagram shows users what content they have engaged with in the past. The quality of such posts has perhaps caught the fancy of users in the past, and they have interacted with it.

- **Relationship:** Users who have become more engaged with your content and have often reacted and looked forward to your post by way of sharing, likes, or comments stand the better chance of seeing your posts.

- **Recent:** Here, we mean that most recent post content will be given priority because it is believed it is likely to perform better in terms of community engagement than stale posts.

But exactly why is timing important? What makes this factor so crucial? Let's examine a few reasons.

You Gain An Edge

You gain an edge if your content is posted at a good time and is most recent. Then there is the highest possible chance that it gets attention. This means that your audience receives your post when they are active, and they are able to see your most recent post (which should ideally be a new post from you).

Have Your Posts Stay on Top Throughout the Day

A correctly timed post receives more engagement from users. This is obviously what you need, to have your post get greater user engagement. By sending your content on your feed at the right time, you stand a chance of seeing your content get bigger hits of engagement as soon as it is possible. The post could remain on top of their feeds all through the day. Besides, you have increased users and community members speaking with you and giving feedback. That has a multiplier effect on your profile, and their eagerness to see and view your net posts increases naturally. That's good for your profile.

Gain Increased Reach Through Popular Stories

Reach is essential. Basically, reach lets you know how many people have seen your post. When you time your post, you can get a lot of audience for it. When you get a lot of audience for it, Instagram notices its relevancy. And when Instagram notices your post, it is available to your audience more frequently. This means that you have a better reach. Take, for example, your stories. Once your Stories are posted on time and shown more recent on your feed, they will remain on top of your feeds, and that gives you the chance to hear from your audience. You do not have to wait endlessly until they come back online and become active again.

Target the Periods Your Followers Are Active Online

It is essential you know exactly when the majority of your followers are always online. You catch your followers in the very act only when you can target when they come online.

One of the best ways you can discover when your users are active is by using the various Instagram tools that were recommended earlier. Additionally, you can also use the technique posted below. They help you analyze your audience and give detailed insights about them. Most particularly, they help you figure out when your audience is most active.

Post when you see a good number of them online. They won't all always be present online simultaneously, but there is a period when most of them will be online. That is the right time to drop the post. And you can be sure your post will be seen, liked and will receive adequate engagement.

Spare enough time to spot those hours when the majority of your followers are active online and capitalize on that time to drop your post.

Can I Know the Peak Online Time Ahead?

Absolutely! You can know the peak time ahead using Ask Instagram. This is the beauty of Instagram. It gives you a solution to all the answers that you need for effective social marketing. To know those peak hours when your followers are always online, here are a few steps that will guide you:

- Go to your Instagram page.

- Click on "Insight."

- Go to *Audience.*

- Scroll down to see which days of the week and approximate time your followers are active online.

However, if you would like to know more detailed insights, then you might have to use the tools recommended earlier.

Now that I know the peak online hours, what's next?

This is a great question to ask. Now that you know when your followers are always online, the next thing you can do to tailor your post times to meet your followers is to do some trial posting. What does that mean? Since testing and experimenting are tools to gauge the effectiveness of your posts. Try to experiment by posting within the Most Optimal Hour. The experimentation is to help you see if there is any significant improvement in the number of engagement rates you receive.

What If I Can't Spot the Peak Time? Use Instagram Analytics

Instagram analytics will help you find out the peak online time. It will help find how many of your followers are pretty active on Instagram. It'll also inform you which of your content has done well within a given time, while also suggesting which time is best to publish.

What do I need to note about Instagram analytics?

- The black circle indicates the period of the week you often post.

- The blue circle indicates your optimal posting times.

- The smaller blue circles show less optimal yet effective posting times.

- You know your analytic outcome by the number of engagements, likes, and comments.

- You may not see data accumulate until after a week. The rule is patience.

What Are Other Ways Available?
- **Check When Others Post:** This is another strategy to know the right time to post. Check if there is anyone in

your network whom you share the same target audience with. The person doesn't have to be a direct competitor, but someone active with a lot of engagement rates. Find out when they post by merely turning on your post notifications.

- **Post for Your Most Active Time zone(s):** Always ensure you use your most active time zone, depending on whether you're aiming at followers within the country, region, or state. Find the best time zone to post.

- **Post During Off-Work Hours:** Instagram users only come online during office hours maybe once in three hours. Always target your post to be after work hours when users will be less busy. Be sure any post during working hours will not get any significant likes, comments, or shares if it gets any at all.

- **Use the Most Important Posts for Weekdays, Not Weekends:** Use the weekdays to engage your B2B companies and the weekends to post to bloggers. Blogging is most times done as a side job, so bloggers are often engaging during the weekends. But be sure that posts for B2B companies are all best done during the week.

What Should You Be Posting?

We have understood the when. Time to understand the what aspect of your posting.

Always keep this at the back of your mind when you're using social media for marketing: It's not much about quantity but quality; not about volume but value.

So, what are the different types of content you can post? Let us look at some of them.

Product User Tutorials

Your customers deserve to know how to use the products they buy from you. You can sometimes push out information regarding the products, especially how users can optimally enjoy them.

GoPro is an incredible account that manages to combine awesome visuals, and at the same time, inspire people in the many ways they can use the product.

What Goes on Without the Products

Once in a while, you can post behind-the-scenes about how certain products are made. But know your niche so that you don't sell your ideas.

HP enjoys showing some behind-the-scenes footage of their events and products occasionally.

Events and Updates

Tell your audience about what upcoming events your company is planning. Keep them updated about sales updates, discounts, special offers, promotions, etc.

Check out Kaspersky Lab's Instagram account to see how they do events. It just makes you excited to see what the team is up to next.

Brand Goals and Vision

Remind your customers about the goal and vision of your company. Not many have the time to visit your website. Keep them in touch with your aspirations.

Chobani has an interesting way to show their brand goals and vision; by including their happy customers in their visuals.

Contest Previews

Instagram offers you the platform to host a contest for your followers. You can bring this idea here and show followers how to enter a contest.

If you are in for contests, PlayStation does it like none other. They come up with creative ways for their users to participate in contests.

Unique Customer Photos

You can take some out and snap with your customers. Upload such photos on your Instagram page and share with your business logo and images.

Want to see the inspiration for customer photos? Then you just have to check out McDonald's Instagram page.

Brains Behind the Brand

Show off the founders of your brand. Don't remain anonymous throughout the year. Let your followers know who is driving what.

The game manufacturing company Ubisoft lets you take a peek at their team and the people who create the product.

Business Achievements and Awards

Instagram is a place to tell your own story. Let your followers know your milestone achievements and awards.

Need to show off your achievements and laurels? Then visit the accounts of popular personalities like Christiano Ronaldo and Leonardo DiCaprio to see how it is done.

Trending Products

Never hide those new arrivals. Let your customers know why they need to visit you.

One of the best ways to show your trending products is to do it the way Adidas does.

Hashtag Posts

You can show off customers or followers who have won your contest and hashtag their photo with the product or prize they won.

Look at Apple's Instagram account and see how they incorporate hashtags into their posts.

Inspirational Post

Inspire your followers with great images and quotes. They are not just buyers; they also need to live. You can show them some love.

One of the best ways to post out inspirational quotes is by using the visuals adopted by popular author Paolo Coelho.

When you combine the above ideas with your content strategy, you will realize that you have so many options to play with. You are practically spoilt for choice.

Story Series

We've already talked about Instagram stories, but you can also create posts that are part of an ongoing series of Instagram stories.

Let's look at how this works by using an example. Imagine that you create shoe art. You have a unique artistic style and you make some of the coolest designs on your shoes. So how do you create a series on it?

Think of your audience. Who would actually purchase shoes that have funky designs on them? Let's say that you target high school and college-aged kids. Your target audience would probably be between 13-24. You've nailed that part. Time to move on to the creative section. What kind of content would your audience like to see? Perhaps they would like to see a series about young sport enthusiasts who use your shoes. That sounds pretty cool.

Now you have the following information.

Content Idea: Sport enthusiasts

People included in the content: Young folks, preferably in the 15-18 year range

The next thing is to decide how often you would like to create a new post in the series. You can choose to post every week or even every day. For this example, let's pick a daily schedule. Here is how this is going to work.

On Day 1, you could show a young boy playing football, wearing one of your awesome shoes.

Day 2 can feature another person simply playing basketball with her friends, showing off another shoe design.

Continue creating your series, adding as many posts as you can.

Having a series can make a great impact on your content. You have identified your audience and you are targeting them with interesting posts.

Trending Topics

Why not hack into a topic that is already trending? When something is already making waves, jump in on the trend bandwagon and use the content to boost your presence. This is a favorite trick used by numerous brands. There are two reasons for using this technique:

- You can easily gain popularity because you are already tapping into the interests of the community. Trending topics bring together a lot of people into one section. When you target that population sub-section, you are essentially targeting a huge, interested population.

- You are showing your audience that you are in touch with the times. You need your focus to be present in the now. People enjoy watching the content of those who adapt to fit the trends of today. Otherwise, you might find your content becoming too old, too fast.

How Often Should You Post?

The seemingly obvious thing to do is to post as often as you can. It is normal to want to put your business out there, and as such, you want your product to be known and seen every minute.

Unfortunately, Instagram does not work that way. Some believe in the rule that states that you should post at least once a day and at most thrice a day. This is simply because some customers might view this as an act of desperation, and, depending on your creative technique, you might bore some easily. You need to be constant in creating techniques that intrigue people to visit your page frequently and be interested in your products. Another reason why you must be careful as to the number of times you post is that you want to be consistent or improve on what you started with. If customers sense your lack of commitment or engagement in marketing your product online, they are likely to lose interest fast, and you won't want that to happen.

Outsourcing Your Content

The faster you recognize the potential of social media, the better. This is to say that the platform is another world entirely; people are always active on Instagram. There is no sleeping time. The world on Instagram is a global village, with constant demand and supply.

The question is: can you keep up? And if your answer is no, there is nothing to be ashamed of; it means you are very realistic, and you are ready to find solutions. Some people are identified as content creators or content managers. Their job description is to make sure your page is attractive and creative. Seek them out for creative marketing techniques to keep your customers interested in your products. Another reason to get help for the management of your Instagram page is the need for customer service. Just like brick and mortar companies, people will call to ask questions, make complaints, demand for products, and make inquiries. It is paramount you have someone taking care of their needs. Failure to be excellent in this field can cost you your clients and give you a bad name.

However, you must preserve your authenticity, what makes your products unique. Sometimes it is difficult to pass your vision and mission to other people working for you, and as a result, you might lose the values of your company.

The good news is that there are a lot of applications that can help in this area. All you need to do is set them up and let them do the posting of content based on a particular schedule you set in place. Easy right?

If you do not see the need to, the following are reasons why you should outsource some of your content:

Mindless Engagement

An efficient manner of growing your page on Instagram is to engage users who are not following you yet. You could equally take advantage of the discover page and like pictures of individuals in niches similar to yours, but this would take a lot of time and effort to get results.

There are numerous apps you can take advantage of, but lots of users do not use these applications correctly. Your audience can easily tell if your page feels robotic and would unfollow without thinking twice. To avert this, either get the services of freelance content creators on platforms like Fiverr or Upwork to help you with content creation. Or you can check out numerous accounts like yours and set-up your chosen service to see what they do to engage with the followers of these pages.

Experienced Help

Sometimes the ability to create unique content sounds foreign. You have no idea how to get captivating images or pictures that can attract your clients or customers. Instead of settling for posts that are of low quality, it is advised that you engage personnel who have the creative ability to make this happen. They will capture images that best represent your products, consequently giving you a professional outlook. Instead of brainstorming on ways you can manage the situation, simply engage an expert.

Time

You do not necessarily have to be on Instagram 24/7 to be highly productive. There are periods of the day when your clients or customers are more active. You can make good use of apps specialized in creating a plan or tracking schedules on when to come online. The alternative is giving the job to another person to do or by using an application. They will have the duty of making sure that post is uploaded promptly, and they are certain to utilize every second of the day.

Hashtag Marketing

One of the major mechanisms of keeping your post in sight is taking advantage of trendy hashtags. This can make your product visible to viewers frequently. The disadvantage of not refreshing your hashtag usage is that other trendy matters will overtake your followers' feeds fast. It is thus vital that you are in sync with is happening and trendy. You must be aware of what people are saying at every particular time. In case other activities and errands restrict you, it is best advised that you outsource your content to someone or using an app that has the primary duty of making sure you appear on every popular hashtag there is.

Where Can I Find People to Outsource My Content?

Now that you know the importance of outsourcing content, you must be wondering where you can find content creators or Instagram managers.

Below are a few top picks:

- Fiver

- Upwork

- Freelancer

- People Per Hour

- Truelancer

Apps That Can Help You in Posting Inspirational Content and Quotes

What if you want to get your followers inspired? You see other brands uploading great visual quotes, and think: Okay, let me try this. What next? All you need to do is get your inspirational juices flowing and get those quotes out, right? Well, you try it out, and you come to a realization: This is not as easy as I imagined!

How come others can make it work when you can't? Easy! Some applications can help you out with it. A few of them are:

- Canva

- Phonto

- InstaQuote

- PicMonkey

- PicLab

- Over

- Typic

Third-Party Apps That You Can Use on Instagram

There are plenty of third-party apps that provide you with

incredible features to enhance your Instagram content game. But the challenge is finding out which ones are right for you. Rather than going through all the apps, why not check out the list below to get some inspiration.

Snapseed

This is a phot-editing tool that provides you with some awesome features to make your photos 'pop.' And the best part? It's free!

Available for both Android and iOS devices you can use both JPG and RAW files. This means that professional photographers can use this software to add final touches to their RAW photo files. You can even remove elements from the photo, adjust the geometry of objects in the photo, control the brightness with precision using the curves feature and so much more. If you would like to have a photo-editing tool ready for use, then this is the one to have.

Layout

This app is specially designed by Instagram to organize your content. If you head over to anyone's account, then you will notice that content is usually arranged in a grid. Each row of the grid contains 3 images. This was a fixed feature on Instagram and you could do nothing to change it.

Until now.

Instead of having a row with three pieces of content, you can have an image that occupies multiple grids. Let me show you what I mean. This is a typical Instagram grid.

Image 1	Image 2	Image 3
Image 4	Image 5	Image 6
Image 7	Image 8	Image 9

With the new layout, here is what you can do.

Image 1	Image 2
Image 3	Image 4
Image 5	

How cool is that? You can merge multiple cells, both horizontally and vertically to create unique layout patterns for your content. Using that, you can easily stand out from the crowd.

LifeLapse

Stop motion can be really fun to experience. This is a unique way to showcase yourself or your products. But the problem with stop motion videos are that they take a long time to make. Even if you have a professional video production team, you might discover that it takes quite a bit of time to create a stop motion video.

For that reason, you now have an app that can help you avoid all the complications that come with creating a stop motion video. Using the app, you can instantly start creating unique content for your audience. Using multiple photos, you can stitch them together through the app and create a video. You can even use a collection of royalty-free music to add a bit more excitement to your content!

Chapter 5:
How to Keep Your Audience Engaged Through Stories and Using Short High-Quality Video

Stories are the new attraction on Instagram. This feature takes the viewers or followers in the life of the business and product. It gives soul to the brand. The introduction of this feature on Instagram takes the viewer a step further into the motion picture of what a company or a brand looks like.

Unlike posting static pictures, videos and stories can take your followers into your day to day life. But similar to pictures, you must be creative to maintain the interest of your followers. It is not acceptable to post anything and everything, as this might mar your brand and might bore your followers. So, what do you do? How can you use short videos or stories? Here are some tips:

Stories are like Snapchat. They create content that is interesting and relatable. This is why it is advised that your stories must be in line and sync with the rest of your brand. Stories are highlighted on your viewer's pages; they last for 24 hours before they are taken down. You can post as much as 12 stories. They can consist of quotes, videos, pictures, and much more. One of the advantages of Stories is that you can save your Stories to your highlights on your main page, which creates a kind of portfolio or profile. It gives your product a vibe of creativity and consistency.

Instagram Stories must be utilized to make a difference in your business. Great use of this feature can increase in your client base, and that is great. It presents you with an opportunity to engage actively with your clients. This is possible through the latest features on Instagram Stories. Next, let us take a look at how you can use Stories to drive engagement.

Ways to Use Stories to Drive Engagement

Polls

This is a perfect feature for business and brands. The reason is that you have the opportunity to ask your viewers about their opinion on a product, subject matter, or a take a vote. This way, you can survey what your users find appealing and what they don't.

Swipe Meter

With the swipe meter, your audience can make suggestions and give their preference for a product above another.

Questions Feature

This is the most interactive of them all. Here you pick a post on your Instagram Story and request that your clients or customers ask you anything. The additional benefit of this is that you can post your answer and the question at the same time so that others will view it. It is brilliant! This way, your clients will be aware of your presence and availability to take them through questions and problems. They will also know that you care about their opinion on how to make improvements and suggestions.

Swipe Up

This is a perfect way to provide more information for your customers. This is the way you refer them to a website. This is perfect for businesses with multiple accounts or websites. Instead of repetition of content, you can request that your customers swipe up on an icon that is usually shown below the screen of your video to access more information. This feature is, however, available to Instagram users who have more than 99,999 followers. It is sort of a special treat for users who have grown their network on Instagram.

Hashtags

Guess what? You can maximize the usage of hashtags even on your Stories, as earlier said, but remember that you have to be trendy so that you can be able to reach a large audience. However, remember that Stories must be in sync with each other, so your hashtag must be in connection with what you are saying.

Shared Posts

You can make your Instagram feed accessible to your viewers on your Stories. Instagram gives you the option of sharing your pictures or videos on your story. Your ability to make good use of your hashtags and other features mentioned above can provide a great marketing scheme for your brand.

Create a Weekly Series

Nothing can be compared to coming across a great piece of material and finding out that it comes from a source with a lot more to offer. Instagram Stories provide an opportunity for you to create a series that can help you keep your audience engaged and make them always come back for more every week.

This fantastic thing is that there is no reason to make it complicated. You can decide to do something as simple as sharing a #MondayMotivation mantra on a Monday or a Thursday restaurant recommendation. In addition to the fact that your audience will always anticipate what you have planned for them, this style of producing contents is simple but not tedious.

Let Your Audience See a Step-By-Step Process

An ideal place to share accurate how-to instructions is most likely not with an Instagram post. However, an Instagram Story can be used to share how-to instructions. Instagram Stories come with features that can be used to show any process in its most detailed form, such as directions for a new recipe. In as much as this is itself good, there is more. These stories can be saved in your highlights. Saving them as highlights allows you to develop a series that your followers can look for whenever they require a reference.

Conduct Mini Interviews

While one of the things you can take advantage of with your Stories to make the world aware of what your brand personality is like, there are still some more things you can do with your stories. You can make use of Stories in sharing tricks, tips, and content that are not originally yours. Are you a food blogger? Do you know a fantastic chef? If so, you can get such chef to share some of their most amazing recipes. If you are fortunate to attend an event that a celebrity guest is also attending, it is okay to inquire from their PR person if you will be allowed to ask the celebrity a couple of questions for the sake of your Stories. You can even go to the extent of developing a series which features interviews with some entrepreneurs.

Design and Distribute Templates

If you want to take part in an activity that is fun and can be shared with your community, all you need to do is to make use of Instagram Story templates!

Instagram Story templates are great points to begin the creation of your stories. They have already created layouts consisting of texts, animations, or graphics which you can seamlessly alter to go with any story.

To get this done, bring up your questions and/or topics, then get to Canvas for design. Once done, you can go ahead and share your story. Templates can be created for literally anything. You can decide to create a love/hate template or any kind that comes to mind. These templates spread fast. This, therefore, makes it vital that you save them in your highlights. You should also place your handle on them. It will ensure people know you are the source when they come across it.

Show Your Audience Behind-the-Scenes Footage

Instagram Stories give us the opportunity to have a better knowledge of the folks we follow on Instagram. It helps to know about their personal lives and their real personalities. If you make use of curated Instagram feeds, you can make use of Instagram Stories in getting details from your behind-the-scenes process. When done, this makes it very easy for you to connect with your followers very personally. If you are not sure how to go about this, you can get started by letting your audience know the processes involved in taking a fantastic shot that you will share on your feed. Another way is to let your audience have an idea of what the energy backstage at a fashion show is.

There are quite a number of ways to make use of your Instagram Stories by telling a story. Some of these ways include letting your audience have an idea of what the energy backstage at a fashion show is.

How to Use Instagram to Grow Your YouTube Audience

As a result of the visual aspects of the platform, it has become easy for bloggers with Instagram accounts to build their fan base and promote their YouTube channels with the use of their accounts. Are you trying to get your blogging or vlogging brand to the next level? Have you just opened an account on Instagram? These tips will be beneficial.

Link to Your Latest YouTube Video in Your Profile

At the moment, it is only possible to have live links in your bio on Instagram. Regardless of this, you still have the freedom to link your latest YouTube video. It is possible to get a lot of people to take a look at your YouTube channel and at the same time, take a look at the pictures and videos you have on your Instagram homepage.

How is this possible? Well, this is simple. Simply post a video clip or a picture. This should be posted with a caption such as, "Want to find out more? Take a look at the link to my YouTube channel in my bio!"

Share Special Content

Do you want your viewers on YouTube to have a purpose for following you on Instagram? Then you will have to provide unique content that they can only see on your Instagram page. You can do this by giving them a tour behind-the-scenes, as suggested earlier, or release a special beauty tip related to some beauty tips that you have given in the past.

You have to make your audience aware of the fact that they will always have access to exclusive contents by following your page on Instagram. If you have a habit of posting exclusive content of good quality, your followers on Instagram will always want to check out your videos. That, however, is not all they will do. They will also check out your YouTube page for a full version of the videos you post.

Brand Your Instagram Photos

If you gain a reputation for sharing images that a lot of people consider to be fun and exciting on Instagram, you can be sure that a lot of people will want to share them. You can get these images to look personal by watermarking them with your brand colors, your logo, or the name of your Instagram handler.

If you get this done, your image will always be recognized even if another person posts it on their page. Once people know you are the source of an image, they can always visit your page for more images like that.

You can also brand your posts by making a custom hashtag. Ensure that all your pictures get tagged with this hashtag, and it will be possible for people to see them via feeds that are not yours. As soon as your hashtag is clicked, all the content you have done can be accessed from that one point.

Chapter 6:
Strategies to Grow Your Following and Audience While Simultaneously Creating Your Brand

A brand is how a firm, a corporation, or an organization is seen by individuals that have come into contact with it first-hand.

A brand is intangible, which is why a brand cannot be defined in the same way as a tangible product. Nonetheless, there are lots of similarities in their definition. It is common knowledge that one characteristic of a sea turtle is the place it lives in. Living in the ocean makes a sea turtle a sea turtle. This is not so different from a brand when looked at fundamentally. If you are to answer the question "What is a brand?" the location of the brand will have to be considered. Brands are located in the minds of people. These people include but are not limited to investors, the media, employees, and most of all, the customers and consumers.

Brands can simply be called perceptions.

How a firm tries to establish its image in the eyes of its customers is simply known as branding.

The implication of this is when firms design websites, which give visitors detailed information about some of the things they offer, they choose certain colors which are associated with their firm, develop ads for promoting services and design a logo and have it featured on all their social media accounts; such firm is undergoing branding. This implies that you are giving people thoughts about what your firm stands for.

What you want your clients to think about your brand might be important. It, however, is nothing compared to what they say about your brand. This is because the reality is what they, the customers, say about your brand. The impression your customers get whenever they come across your brand is what matters. This impression is dependent on whatever they feel when they come across you.

What Is the Importance of a Brand?

Some firms are reluctant to invest in branding. This reluctance occurs as a result of perception. Not every firm knows how to relate profit in business with branding. Regardless of this, being able to develop a great brand is priceless.

What is the point of investing in branding? The key word in this sentence is "investment." Not a lot of organizations view branding as an investment; this is actually where they start getting it wrong. Firms that have an understanding of the role branding plays in influencing the behavior of customers to know that branding is more than just any strategy. Branding is a special strategy which can go a long way in determining the success level of a company. Big returns can be had from investing in branding.

Let's go through some of the most notable returns that a firm can get from investing in branding.

Attract the Right Customers

Customer research is an integral part of branding. Online surveys, focus groups, and interviews make it possible for firms to find out what type of customers are best for your firm's values as well as their purposes. Access to this information makes it much easier to create great audience personas. It also makes it easy for firms to develop marketing messages that are targeted to a firm's ideal customer. Now there is a considerable likelihood that your ideal customers will patronize you. That is, however, not all they would do. They are also very likely to stay loyal to your brand over a long period of time. There are few things that offer more value than brand loyalty.

Enhance Marketing Effectiveness

If you want an easy way to make your efforts in marketing effectiveness. A well-articulated and cohesive brand brings about marketing initiatives that are cohesive and well-articulated. Branding covers brand personality and core messaging.

With the right customer research, it is possible to create marketing campaigns that customers most valuable to your brand will find very relevant. As a result of bold new identities, marketing touch points become engaging.

Close Deals With Less Difficulty

If you talk to a salesperson about what selling entails, what they'll tell you is that brands that are well defined and strategically positioned can be sold very easily. The reason for this is because they have their value propositions attached to their brand narrative. With branding, your sales team has a better advantage, which goes a long way in making it easy for them to bring deals to a closure confidently and quickly.

Command Higher Prices

The saying, "Customers do not buy products. They buy brands," is important. It is not a break from the norm for customers to be ready to pay enormous prices for whatever brands they consider to be superior. If you purchase a blue t-shirt from Gucci, you will probably have to part with over $100. However, if you buy that same t-shirt from Hanes, you will only pay about $5. With the right level of branding, your firm can occupy a premium position in whatever industry you are in and can have value propositions which no other firm in your industry can boast of. With this, you can be sure of a generally accepted high worth, which gives you the freedom to attach a huge price tag on your products.

Boost Business Value

The strength of brand equity cannot be overestimated. Brand equity does not only serve as justification for an increase in price points; it also affects your share price positively. Usually, stronger financial performances are associated with stronger brands. When branding is taken advantage of for an extended period, it has a good effect on your company's worth when it's time to exit. When a firm invests in branding, it can enjoy returns of high value when it's time to make negotiations about a selling price.

How Millennials Are Buying From Firms That Put Emphasis on Branding

Before getting into what millennials expect and desire, it is vital that we have a full understanding of who millennials are.

Who Exactly Are Millennials?

Millennials are individuals that were born between the years of 1977 and 2000. They are up to 25% of the population of the United States. That is not all. They also make up 21% of consumer discretionary purchases.

Although a lot of people consider millennials to be a group of carefree and restless teenagers, the truth is that this group of people are not as young as they used to be. A lot of them have now become parents.

What Millennials Want

At this point, to a large extent, we know who exactly millennials are. Now that we know who millennials are, we need to pay attention to what their needs, expectations, wants, and desires are in regard to the way they interact with brands.

Although this group of people that are regarded as millennials can be referred to as a broad-ranging group, there are some desires that they jointly share

Convenience

Millennials were brought up in an environment in which convenience is a keyword. They are used to phenomenon such as video streaming, fast foods, and personalized social media feeds. Millennials are used to getting answers to whatever questions they have by asking Google.

They have a mindset of judging things by how efficient, available, and fast, those things are. Firms that have been able to recognize this feature of millennials have been able to offer convenience to millennials successfully.

In as much as there is a lot of proof of the desire of millennials for speed and convenience, one of the most outstanding proofs of the desire of millennials for convenience is the constant drive for same-day grocery delivery. According to reports from MarketBeat, Walmart is undergoing expansion in its same-day online grocery to up to 100 metro areas. This will roughly cover about 40% of the households in the United States as of January 2019.

The fact that millennials are okay with outsourcing and automating a phenomenon as common as purchasing groceries means they will be interested in ways in which they can get in touch with your products more conveniently. If you can find ways of meeting this need, you will be able to make more gains.

Choices

If there is one thing that millennials are used to, it is having a range of choices. In most parts of their lives, millennials can make a lot of choices. When they want to purchase a product, they get the exact product they think they want and then compare it to the same product produced by a lot of other brands. They also have more than one way to pay for products that they want to purchase.

As a result of the availability of lots of choices, consumers now feel like they are in charge. To have millennial customers on your side, you have to make choices available to them. Although this applies to different industries differently, it is a necessity irrespective of your industry.

Experiences

The generations before the millennials were more interested in purchasing commodities. However, millennials are more interested in purchasing experiences.

Are you in the sale of tangible products? You need to go beyond the sale of products. You have to come up with methods to tell an engaging story. Certain firms achieve this by getting their brands aligned with social causes. Some others take advantage of local events to achieve this. What has to be done is to discover something that puts people in one place for bonding.

Budget Friendliness

Millennials are not known for being good managers of money. They have made a couple of financial mistakes in the course of a lifetime. Sometimes, these mistakes are their fault entirely. Other times, they are not to blame. The truth remains that millennials do not have so much money to throw around.

Millennials are not known to make a lot of money. This is in addition to the fact that they have substantial unsettled debt. Millennials spend most of their earnings on things such as cell phone services, groceries, eating out, fueling their cars, seeing movies, and buying gas. As a result of this, they might not have enough money for the product you intend to sell to them.

An understanding of this will help businesses that sell products that are budget friendly; cheaper versions of other expensive product do better among millennials that those that do not.

Belonging

Millennials always want to feel like they are part of something. They will go to great lengths to build connections with various people.

Quite a number of brands have been able to take advantage of the desire of millennials to be part of something. One of these brands is Toms Shoes.

Toms Shoes began with a special business model that gave millennials the feeling that they were influential. It, however, went on to become something huge. At a point, owning a pair of Toms became a symbol of social status.

Services, Software, and Agencies That Can Grow On Autopilot

Creating a stable audience on social media is a great way to make sales and meet potential buyers. This is why established businesses and top companies invest in providing results through the utilization of various Instagram tools available — interested in some of these tools? That is what we will be covering in this section.

Some of these tools include:

Magic Social

This tool is different and unique from every other tool on Instagram because of its peculiarity and special features. Through Magic Social, you can choose your preferred audience without an intervention of any kind. It utilizes and focuses on the demographic pattern of Instagram users, and you also get the opportunity of selecting who you want to follow on Instagram. The tool is needed to create a significant number of followers.

Owlmetrics

Owlmetrics is best utilized for surveying as a marketer on Instagram, it is paramount to analyze the strength of your contents. This tool helps in tracking closely your accomplishments or how far you have come. It monitors your viewer growth and the posts most liked. As a marketer, you will be able to analyze data on the response of your customers online. The reviews help in creating more suitable products, customer services, and content production. This tool also helps in determining the perfect time to post or upload content as interpreted by the tool's analytical feature.

Visco

Nothing is more appreciated on Instagram than nicely and neatly displayed creative content. Instagram is attributed to beautiful pictures and well-edited videos. You gain more followers once it is perceived that your art is genuine and significant. To successfully achieve great picture qualities, you should own a camera and any other relevant instrument.

However, if you don't have any of these instruments, VISCO is the most appropriate application to download in other to achieve the same results. This tool presents a user-friendly technique on how to use the application. With the editing of pictures and videos, you will produce amazing quality pictures for your followers.

Iconosquare

This tool closely monitors the performance of a post. Its analytical features track the most minimal content additions that resulted in a breakthrough of a business or market mechanism. This could be through a tag, a hashtag, or a repost. Whatever it is, Iconosquare fetches it. This is also very handy for Marketers to successfully streamline what works for the audience and does not.

Planoly

Time is always of the essence. The job of uploading and creating a post can take up an entire day, leaving you little or no time to focus on other things. The advantage of Planoly tool is that it gives you the opportunity of scheduling your posts ahead of time. All you have to do is prepare what you intend on sharing and schedule it for a particular time. On the chosen day, you will only use its option to upload immediately. This way, you have adequate time to achieve other things.

FameBit

There are people called brand Influencers. They are mostly bloggers or well-known and established persons who can rightly influence a product or a brand. However, it is difficult to find an influencer who can rightly represent the brand and be authentic in their presentation. Famebit is an application that registers influencers who are eager to utilize great platforms. The application will make visible the budget and campaign available for the project. This helps marketers and influencers easily connect in accordance with the listed factors.

Juicer

Many established business owners or marketers make use of Instagram to complement other platforms, such as their official websites. These platforms are used to build up followers and create awareness of the brand. Juicer, as a tool aids in the compilation or accumulation of Instagram feeds on the official website. Consequently, those visiting the web page are most likely to view the Instagram account. The primary advantage of Juicer is that it uploads automatically on the web page when a post is uploaded.

Linktree

Normally, Instagram users are allowed to click one link to have access to the stipulated address. However, Linktree has made access to more than one link possible. This way, you can link on a specific page and not necessarily the homepage of the website. A major addition to this tool is that it is free and can be used by anybody.

Grum

There are times when content is created on a desktop, but it is difficult to access on a mobile or tablet. This tool makes it possible to post content on your desktop without any difficulties. It allows the user to schedule their content ahead of time.

Ink361

Through Ink361, you can successfully manage your Instagram content and also track how well you are doing, plus you can also check out what others who are in similar line with you are up to. The application is open to all type of users, and it is free. So, if you are starting up on Instagram as a blogger or marketer, you can start with Ink361 since you do not have to pay for the application.

Woobox

Instagram or any other social media presents a perfect platform to gain followers by giving away prizes and holding competitions. Followers are generally known to love freebies, and marketers are more than happy to take full advantage of this trend and build their audience. To accomplish this, Woobox makes it possible to customize competitions between followers with the aim of winning a giveaway prize.

AutoHash

Hashtags are one of the most beneficial features to utilize on Instagram. This is because through hashtags your feeds can be visible in a most unlikely page. There are millions of hashtags on Instagram, and the question is how one can streamline a hashtag that is beneficial to their product, brand, and business.

This is where AutoHash comes into play. Out of the hundreds and thousands of hashtags, this tool streamlines the useful hashtags that correspond to what you need and the kind of audience you will want to follow you.

Kicksta

This tool is a shortcut for getting followers; all you have to do is to register the handle of the people you are interested in following. Kicksta will then like their post. Their natural response would be to follow back. This is advantageous because you do not have to do the work; all you need to do is submit the names of the users you desire to follow you.

Chapter 7:
How to Create and Turn Your Audience Into Clients

You have now implemented a strategy that is ready to propel your Instagram account to new heights.

You are ready to get with the times and adopt the latest trends. Your customers are now active on your Instagram account, and you have begun to gain a steady increase in your following. So now what?

What is your next move going to be?

The number of followers has been increasing, but your sales are not showing the increase that you had hoped they would or alternatively, they have just plateaued. What just happened?

When you end up in a similar position, then here is what you should know, just because someone follows you on Instagram does not mean they are automatically your customer. They could be simply interested in the content that you share on Instagram. In which case, you really are creating interesting content, not sellable content. That does not mean you have to sell in every content you post. You are creating an identity on Instagram; you are forcing a sales pitch on your audience.

Successful businesses know how to turn their followers into customers. Sure, social media is great for brand awareness, but that's useless if it's not leading to conversions.

Now let's look at a surprising fact: Less than 55% of all Instagram users follow brand profiles; more than 60% are curious about products and services via Instagram, while a little above 70% take action thereafter.

You need to get your audience to take actions on your post.

Actions expected of the users include visiting your website, carrying out further searches, shopping with you, or telling a friend about your products and services. You'll need to tap straight into the sales conversion power of Instagram by ensuring you drive traffic to your site and engage your followers.

So how do you do that?

You need to share, not sell.

Why My Business?

What is great about your business? What makes you unique? What kind of personality are you bringing into the products and services?

The idea behind asking these questions is to share what makes your brand great. You have to bring your stories to life. Stories that speak about your product. Stories that show just how your business model works. Stories that reveal how you give your heart into making the stuff that you do.

When people buy stories, they empathize. When they empathize, they understand your business and eventually become loyal followers.

When they start following and trust your business stories, they are encouraged to make purchases of your products.

Share Your "Shoppable" Ideas

Instagram is built with an e-commerce tool named "shoppable Instagram," that helps your followers to be able to see all your product images. All they need do is to click from your profile link through an integrated tool named Yotpo. Yotpo is an Instagram-enabled marketing tool that helps social media marketers to collate and publish verified reviews of products by customer. Yotpo powers the Shoppable Instagram catalog, which serves as an interface that looks like Instagram itself. What that does for you is to increase your social media proof, making your customers feel secure and satisfied while giving sales satisfaction to your brand.

By a simple addition, you are able to create a unique experience to your customers and audiences.

Share CTAs

CTA means "call to action," and it's answering one simple question: What do visitors see first when they're come to my Instagram and look at all the products I have to offer? If those short phrases about what products and services you offer are not catchy, then it's self-defeating. Yes, Instagram deals with visuals, but appealing CTAs enable visitors to cut short unnecessary time spent reading product descriptions. Customers want to know what steps to take to use a product or what solution such products bring to the table in short, simple, catchy phrases. Never undermine this role of CTA. CTAs increase your sale experience. You can use either the third-party apps to create a CTA or through manual linking, captioning, or updating. All of these will optimize your experience.

How Often Do I Show Off My Fans?

Never be in the habit of hiding those who have dedicated their shopping life to your brand. Always show them off for other customers to see and perhaps be won over to your brand. After all, all you need is to increase sales and expand your customer base. Adopting the system of making your customer promote your brand will help connect your customers straight to your brand. Showing customers off gives them a tremendous sense of belonging. They want to identify with your brand and feel connected to it. It is easy to do. Simply tie this to a contest and make sure winners are displayed on your feed and timeline of Instagram and other social media channels you use to market your brand and products. Instagram specifically has the leverage you can use to create great content and share it quickly and to multiple audiences.

Why Not Tell a Story by Showing It?

Remember that previously we stated that people are more at home with visuals rather than the text or audio. More importantly, make sure the content you're sharing is not saying what users can find anywhere. Carve it in a story or testimony format. Don't use the regular method of just writing everything in the usual way. Create a unique niche. Create in a video form such that everyone who watches it can share and recommend it. Here's the rule: Never exaggerate your story. Make it believable.

Using Storytelling in Business Promotion? That Doesn't Sound Believable

It is not strange to hear this kind of assertion in the business circle, especially among naive newbies and start-ups. You don't have to be a film director, scriptwriter, or an artist to be able to write an attractive story. Telling a business's story, especially on a platform like Instagram is like recasting different daily experiences and interactions you have with your customers and brand competitors. Remember, we said that to arouse the emotions of your clients and customers, you need to tell a story around your brand. This will keep them coming again and again.

Creating an Appealing Story

For some people, telling great stories comes naturally to them. They easily put down every experience they have in their brains as stories. They also have no issues recollecting them in an appealing and fun manner.

If you are in this category, great for you, however, for those of us who are not, we need to put in some more effort.

What you require under your belt is a bunch of amazing stories. Think of what is happening around you. See if you have any updates. Or look at your products and see if there is an interesting way to communicate them to the audience.

Okay, I am going to bring back the example of GoPro right here (not because I am biased towards them). They showcase stories of their customers. They show what their customers are doing around the world using GoPros.

They rarely sell, unless they have a new product or model that they launch into the market.

What stories can you say about your products?

Let us assume that you make doughnuts. Then perhaps your stories could include the way in which people enjoy your doughnuts. Show off families having your doughnuts in your outlet. Have your customers take pictures with your staff. When you tell a story, you are creating a narrative that people can empathize with.

In the example of the doughnut shop above, you are basically creating this impression in their minds: "Hey, have you seen that doughnut shop? It looks like it is a fun place to be for families."

Then, you can pick from the stories in your arsenal as you require to fit the specific situation you believe would be interesting and useful to your prospective client.

You can utilize this story in your introduction or when the target client speaks about a specific problem they are dealing with. To create the stories, you need first to consider the common issues your service or product can solve. Next, think of instances where customers faced this specific issue.

After you have covered that, you need to put down a brief paragraph which summarizes the example. Below are a few tips that can be of assistance:

- Let it be a personal story. Ensure you don't speak about an organization. Speak about an actual person who was dealing with an issue that your service or product fixed. This way, the prospect will be able to relate to your story more because it seems real. This is not all; your target client will feel more compassion towards an individual as opposed to an organization.

- First, speak about the issues the person dealt with; ensure you make efforts to describe them using personal terms. This way, the prospect would be able to relate to your story. Make the person the hero of your story. They dealt which an issue which they were able to overcome by working alongside you.

- Don't focus too much on what your service or product did: Although you may find this fun, you may not be able to say the same about your prospect. In fact, to them, this is the area they would find the least entertaining. They have more interest in if the issue you fixed relates to yours and the benefits or value your solution provided.

- Use the benefits your products or service offered as your closing: This is a critical step. However, you need to do this as naturally as possible. Don't make it seem like the value provided by your product was a rare occurrence. Make it seem like it is an aspect of your daily business.

Put down these examples using conversational and natural language. Then go through it until it begins to sound correct. Next, practice the core points, so it does not seem scripted.

Action Stages in the Strength Of Storytelling

- Tell a story that shows the value and establishes a connection.

- Your persuasive story signifies to the buyer that it is secure in approaching.

- Create trust and rapport so the buyer will not forget for a long time.

- Watch out for signs of cooperation

- Close the sale.

People desire happiness. If they can see themselves being happy with their choices, they will purchase from you. When you create compelling stories that let your clients incorporate themselves in the story, they will be able to relate and establish their own powerful and similar imagination. They will have no other option than to go further.

Leveraging the strength of storytelling is not always straightforward and requires a tremendous amount of practice. However, doing it will ensure your job is more entertaining and will enhance your success rate.

Chapter 8:
Using Instagram Ads for Maximum Reach

Instagram Advertising: What Is It?

Instagram Advertising is a way user pay to post sponsored images or videos on Instagram. This is done to reach a more targeted, broader audience. Although an individual or organization may decide to run adverts for a host of reasons, Instagram adverts are frequently utilized in growing traffic on websites, brand exposure, generating new leads and moving existing leads into the funnel and converting them to actual clients.

Instagram is a platform that works using visuals, and for this reason, text ads would not work. Instead, you require images or videos which you can support with text to get to your audience using Instagram ads.

The great part? Advertising on Instagram does work. As stated by Instagram, 60% of individuals said they discovered new products via the platform, while 75% of Instagram users take action after a post inspired them.

Just like running ads on Facebook, backing up a post with more cash will result in more brand exposure. It will also offer you more control over the individuals who will be able to view your post.

Is Advertising on Instagram the Best Route for Your Business?

To get an answer to this, you need to answer some questions:

- Who are the individuals on Instagram?

- Are they an older population, or are you targeting a younger generation of customers?

- Are they uploading pictures of their pets or kids?

If this does not seem like the audience you want to target, it does not mean you should not take a look into this platform. This is because more adults past the ages of 34 will probably begin to take advantage of the platform as it keeps growing. Also, if your aim is the adults over the ages of 65, you will have the capacity to target this demographic directly.

Just like a host of other platforms for social advertising, Instagram offers you the opportunity to target specific age ranges, behaviors, interest, genders, and locations, among others. You will also have the capacity to target a custom audience. This will ensure that you show your ads to just your list of prospects or those that have a makeup similar to them.

Instagram utilizes the demographic data of Facebook to send ads to the right parties. This makes it a tool that is very valuable for advertisers and brands who have the goal of targeting a niche audience. This is because Facebook already has extensive demographic targeting options.

If you are in a creative or visual sector like selling footwear or in the restaurant business, Instagram advertising can be a really powerful tool.

Instagram ads are improving year after year. Presently, the tool is powerful and gives you access to a huge population. But that's not all that it does. Here are some other advantages that you can get from using ads on Instagram.

Targeting Options

2019 showed Instagram introducing better targeting options on its platform. This has allowed people to reach out to the audience that they want. There are still certain limitations in the targeting, but the options Instagram already provides is more than enough to satisfy the goals of most businesses and brands. Why is this beneficial to you, apart from marketing your products to the people who care about it the most?

For one, you can actually avoid reaching out, and paying for advertising to audiences who are not interested in your product. In other words, you have a better chance of translating your audience to customers or sales. Currently, you can use various targeting options such as location, automated targeting, demographics, custom audiences, interesst, behaviors, and look alike audiences.

What are custom audiences? Let's say that you want to target two different groups of people. One group contains people aged between 21-30 who live in one city while the other group, also falling in the same age criteria, live in another city. Before, you had to create two different advertisements to separately target the two cities. But now, you can create a custom audience and add both cities to your targeting list. Simple isn't it?

Look alike audience is another cool feature in Instagram ads. Imagine that you have tested your advertisements in 3 cities, City A, City B, and City C. You realize that the audience for City C has generated the most revenue. Now you would like to replicate the success you had in City C in City D. Rather than creating a campaign all over again, you can use a look alike audience to target City D with the same audience criteria you had used for City C.

With greater targeting ability, you can make sure that you are creating ad campaigns that are customized to the region, country, and even city, allowing you more flexibility in your ads.

Unique Type of Ads

Instagram has increased the type of ads that you can see on the platform. You can use photos, videos, carousels, stories, and collections type of ads on the platform. Collections is especially unique because it allows you to create ads that look like product catalogs! This means that rather than developing your own catalog, you can make use of the template already provided by Instagram. Add in your product pictures, write a cool description about your product, then add the price and you are good to go! If people interact with your ad, you can direct them to your website or you can take them to a special purchase page within Instagram itself. You don't need to have special knowledge to work with the ads. They are easy to figure out and you might just find yourself pushing out cool ads in no time.

Ad Objectives

Instagram noticed that it could actually provide advertisers with the ability to promote their products or services better by offering them the option of picking their ad objectives. These ad objectives that are available on Instagram can be used to synchronize with the business goals that you have established. For example, if you are looking to get more views for your video, you can let Instagram know and it will try and find audience for that. If you are looking for conversions, then Instagram's AI can help you with that. The results are not 100 percent precise, but they take in years and years of data available on Instagram to provide you with better targeting options.

What Is the Cost of Instagram Ads?

The cost of Instagram ads is dependent on a range of factors. It uses cost per impression (CPM) and cost-per-click (CPC) models. It determines its pricing using Instagram's ad auction.

The great news is that you are able to control the allocation of your budgets. For example, you can decide to go with a daily budget, which would restrict the amount you spend daily. You could equally decide to go with a lifetime budget, where you create ads that will run for a period until you deplete your budget.

Other methods of regulating the way your Instagram ad spends funds include setting the schedule of your ad. For example, you can state specific hours daily you would like your ads to run.

You can also set up the delivery method for your ad. Here, you would be able to choose between impressions, link clicks, and unique daily reach.

Lastly, you can set your bid amount. You have the option of choosing between automatic or manual.

Steps to Take Before You Begin Running Ads on Instagram

It may initially seem complicated to learn the intricacies of running ads on Instagram. However, the great news is that if you have run ads on Facebook previously, there is not a lot for you to learn. You can run Instagram ads via the Facebook Ads Manager.

However, if you are new to it entirely, it is not an issue. We will be looking at the process below. You also have the option of creating some straightforward ads using straight from the Instagram application.

If you are a more advanced advertiser or you want to run a vast ad set, you have the choice of configuring your ads using the Marketing API of Facebook or the Power Editor. For brands who need to purchase and manage numerous ads, provide content at scale, and manage a vast community, they can take advantage of Instagram Partners.

Now, let us take a look at how you can create an ad using the Facebook Ads Manager. It is very common because it is easy to use. It also gives users the capacity to customize these ads better than you would be able to do using the application itself.

So how do you create a new Instagram ad? Below are the steps to note:

Head to the Facebook Ad Manager

To get to the Facebook Ads Manager, use this link:

https://www.facebook.com/business/tools/ads-manager

Note that this is under the assumption that you are logged into the right Facebook account.

Note that Instagram does not have any actual Ads Manager. You manage your Instagram ads using the Facebook Ads UI.

Set Up Your Marketing Goals

Here, you choose your campaign objective. This is listed in a manner that is easy to understand. Need more reach? Pick the reach goal. In search of more traffic? Pick the traffic goal, and so on.

However, you need to note that Instagram ads will only function with the goals below:

- App installs

- Brand awareness

- Engagement

- Traffic

- Reach

- Video views

- Conversions

Set Up Your Target Audience

Just like Facebook, you will be able to set up a targeted audience for your ad campaigns. There are numerous options for segmentation, which include:

- Age

- Location

- Custom Audiences

- Behaviors

- Demographics

- Lookalike

- Connections

- Interests

Lots of advertisers fail to spend enough time here. The result of this is an excessively broad audience, which makes your brand exposed to lots of individuals who don't find your brand relevant. Others may make the mistake of overusing this capacity and use lots of precise targeting options, which results in a very small audience.

The right thing to do is create a balance. The significant part is that doing this is not difficult. When you are trying to configure your Instagram Ad campaign via the ad platform offered by Facebook, there is a handy guide which gives you the ability to check if you made your audience too specific or broad. Your goal should be in the center of the green zone to get the appropriate number of significant individuals.

If you have previously utilized this for Facebook Ads, then you would probably have developed lots of audiences, and this process will not be not new to you. However, for first-timers, you will be provided with a rundown of your targeting choices, which you will be able to set to attain a specifically targeted audience.

For example, if your target is men in Los Angeles who fall within the ages of 20 and 35, who have an interest in gaming and fitness, you would be able to do just that.

The instant you are done configuring your audience, Facebook will offer you a guide to how broad or specific your audience is.

It is crucial you pay attention to this tool because you don't want your audience to be too large or too specific.

Pick Your Placements

Now that you are targeting the demographic you desire, the next step is to pick your placements. This is essential if your campaign objective is only to run ads on Instagram. If you decide to skip this step, Facebook will let your ads run on the two platforms.

This may not be a bad thing; however, if the content you developed is for Instagram precisely, you need to pick "Edit Placements" here.

From this location, you will be able to pick the placement as Instagram. You will also be able to decide if you want these ads to show up in the stories or feeds area of the platform.

Set Your Ad Schedule and Budget

If you are not familiar with how budgets work on other platforms for advertising, then this may come with a bit of trial and error. When running your first ad campaign on Instagram, you can decide to run a lifetime or daily campaign. This is dependent on which best suits your needs.

The great part, however, is that you can stop or pause your campaign at any moment if you believe your budget is not being allocated properly.

Develop Your Instagram Ad

At this stage, you need to create your ad on Instagram.

By now, you should already know the kind of content you want to promote. Depending on the campaign goals you may have, this aspect may seem different from that of other advertisers or brand.

However, you will need to know that Instagram ads have different formats. You will always have the option of selecting from the formats below:

- Image Feed Ads

- Video Story Ads

- Image Story Ads

- Carousel Feed Ads

- Video Feed Ads

- Canvas Story Ads

Best Practices for Advertising on Instagram

The following are some of the top practices to follow, which can help you create fantastic Instagram ads:

Let Every Ad Have Some Personality

Irrespective of if this is an emotional video, or a funny joke or an image that showcases your culture, if your post on Instagram seems robotic then you may be unable to reach your potential for engagement.

Lots of people head to Instagram either to be amazed, have fun, or to laugh. No one heads to Instagram to watch a boring advert of your brand. That is why it is crucial to appeal to emotions.

Ensure Your Ad Is Relevant to the Platform

What may work on Twitter will most likely not work on Instagram. This is because audiences on each platform have different thought patterns.

You need to place yourself in the shoes of your target buyer and know where they are. Your target is most likely not going to read two pages of text on Instagram. You need to make sure your ads don't seem sales-driven because this is not what Instagram is best for.

Take Advantage of Hashtags

Try to add a bit of creativity with your hashtags. Do a little bit of research to find out the hashtags your audience tends to search for. Also, remember not to use hashtags excessively. It can result in your post looking desperate and sloppy.

Run a Contest

Running a giveaway or contest is one of the best methods of attaining your goals quicker using Instagram advertising. This is because individuals enjoy free things as well as competition. This is such a great way of sparking excitement about your brand in your audience.

Post During Peak Hours

To post during peak hours, you can take advantage of the ad schedule feature Instagram offers. However, this is a feature you can get only if you use a lifetime budget. It's a fantastic way to reaching people at the appropriate time.

If you understand your audience, it should not be difficult to determine this. However, trial and error are also effective here.

If you sell laptops, what days do you experience the most spike in traffic? If you own a restaurant, when do people typically order for meals? Providing answers to these questions is the best place to begin.

Tap Into Your Analytics

Now that Instagram has removed the likes feature from your posts, it has become even more important to tap into your analytics and find out more about how your posts are performing and exactly what you should be doing in order to attract more engagement to your content. But don't look at just engagement. If you are posting a video, look at the drop-off rate. This will let you know the average watch time of your videos, allowing you to make informed decisions based on the numbers. Are your videos too long? Are people getting bored of the long intro you have added to those videos? Each and every metric is important.

In a similar manner, tap into your metrics to discover what kind of content is popular among your audience. Check your stories to see if you are showing growth in your views. If there is no increase in the number of views, then your stories are not capturing the attention of your audience properly.

How to Create a Brand-Specific Product

To create a product specific to your Instagram brand, which you would be able to sell using various drop-shipping methods, the guidelines below can be of help:

Decide What You Want Customers to Know You For

You don't want to focus on the parts of your brand your competition surpasses you. Instead, you want to pay attention to those areas that make you more enticing. The core differentiator of your brand should be significant to your clients. Determine what you want people to link you with and pick up from there.

Don't Forget to Research

This may not seem like fun but doing research will aid you in aligning your business offers with the needs and wants of your prospects. If will also let you know the areas you need to sort out before your product is more enticing to your audience.

A simple method of doing this could be to carry out an Instagram poll. Let your followers vote on aspects of your product you can change that they would love. This way, when you develop the product, you will be sure there is already a market.

Determine Your Differentiators

You may decide to go with one differentiator for your product or more. However, anyone you decide to go with must help your product be specific to your brand.

Reach Out to Your Manufacturer

After determining the differentiators, you want to make use of, reach out to your producer to help you create your product.

Connect With Your Target

Now, you can begin sharing the story of your brand specific product around the world. Take in orders and ensure you already have a method of getting your product to the final consumers who may require your product.

Importance of Creating a Brand Specific Product

A brand specific product is one you can utilize in separating your product from other products on offer in the market or on platforms like Instagram. Irrespective of your business size, or the industry you belong in, you need to create a product specific to your brand which offers you a competitive advantage in the market.

If you are not still convinced as to why you need a product specific to your brand; the following are some of the benefits you stand to gain;

- Show Your Brand's Value: By making a product which is unique to your brand, you can showcase the value of your brand in a range of areas. These could include ethics, customer service among a host of others.

- Highlight Your Unique Selling Point: By creating a brand specific product, you will be able to draw focus to the value of your brand is providing. You will also be able to let customers know that there is no alternative available to the product you are providing. Even though your competitors may offer products that seem like yours, the experience you are providing is unique.

- Enhance Brand Loyalty: Lastly, by creating a great product which is specific to your brand, it will enhance customer loyalty.

- Help your clients see the features that make your brand what it is.

How to Contact a Manufacturer to Create a Differentiated Product

Now that you have gotten this far, now it is time to reach out to a manufacturer to produce your differentiated product. How do you go about this? This is what we will be covering in this section. But first, let's take a run through the basics of product differentiation.

Product Differentiation; What Does it Mean?

Product differentiation, which is sometimes known as differentiation is a process of marketing where an organization differentiates a service or product from other similar ones in the market. The aim of this is to make it more enticing to the target market.

It has to do with clearly stating the unique position of the offering in the market. This is possible by elaborating the distinct advantages it offers to the target audience. It may also be classified as stating the product's distinct selling proposition to make it different from the others on the market.

Why Is Product Differentiation Crucial?

Now, there is a lot of competition in the market between various brands. This has resulted in a division of demand among the leading players. For this reason, it has become crucial for brands to help their customers the unique benefits they stand to gain from purchasing their products.

Asides from ensuring the product lasts in the market, product differentiation is crucial for a lot of reasons. Below are a few of them:

- Product differentiation transforms the attributes of the

product into advantages.

- It helps in answering the most crucial question of customers – what do I stand to gain?

- It offers the clients a reason to buy the product of the brand and continue purchasing in the future.

- It enhances the product's recall value.

- It develops brand equity and enhances brand loyalty.

Now, let us take a look at some methods of differentiating your product.

Methods of Differentiating Your Products

You don't want to make a product that is different just because you want it to be. Rather, you need to put those things that are important to your customers into consideration. These are the factors you will use in pushing your differentiation choices.

Your product differentiation should come up after you have done elaborate research on what your competition is doing. It should be an aspect of a broader product vision.

Below are a few ways you can differentiate your product. They include:

Value

What benefits can clients expect from utilizing your service or product in comparison to the competition? What issue is the product going to help fix? How is it going to better the lives of the customers and make it easier?

For instance, your product may be the only one available that helps users charge their phones daily when there is no source of power available.

Design

Do you have a product which comes in a design that makes it unique from others? For instance, your product is smaller and easy to use, while that of the competition is very complex to use and very large.

This difference may aid clients in creating a connection with your brand. By using fresh designs, even while using old concepts, your organization would be able to make its product stand out. In turn, your organization would attain a competitive advantage.

Price

Do you have a product which comes at a price higher or lower than the products your competitors offer? Your price should show the kind of value your product provides.

For instance, you can validate a higher price if clients are aware that your product provides unique quality. This is the way luxury brands like Gucci can command top prices for their products. However, if your asking price is too little, customers may not believe your product is actually of value.

Product Quality

Do you have a product which is just better than what your competitors offer? Do you provide a certain feature which your competitors don't have? Is your product more durable than other similar products?

The competitive advantage of your product may be its superior dependability and construction.

Customer Service

Your product may have numerous features similar to others in numerous ways. But you will be able to differentiate the experience customers have with your product. You can make this possible by creating an efficient support team and getting status for being responsive to the idea, needs, and requests of customers.

The method you decide to go with when differentiating your products should not be a response to the activities your competitors are engaged in. Rather, it should come from a strategy of objectives specific to your business, services, and products.

Picking a Manufacturer to Contact: Domestic or Overseas?

The first thing you need to do is to determine the kind of manufacturer you are in search of. With a quick search on the net, you will find a broad range of options to pick from. However, before doing this, you need to determine the kind of manufacturer you have an interest in working alongside. Do you want a domestic manufacturer, or someone based overseas?

- Domestic: if the manufacturer creates products in the country you reside in, he/she is domestic.

- Overseas: A manufacturer who resides outside the country you live in is overseas.

Getting Ready for Manufacturing:

Before you hire a manufacturer and begin to manufacture your product, there are some steps you need to take before you begin.

They include:

- Carry Out Market Research. Do not manufacture a product your customers don't want to buy. Take a look at other competitors to have an idea of how your product offers extra benefits to your customers. If you create a product version, which is worse than the product your competitors produce, you are most likely going to be unsuccessful.

- Get The Proper Licensing. Next, you need to determine if you want to manufacture the product and sell on your own or license the concept to an organization that has the experience and means of handling it.

- Licensing Is Similar to Tenting Your Idea. The organization deals with all aspects of the product ranging from the: production, distribution, and marketing. Then the company pays you royalties depending on how much they sell. You do not need to make any investment ahead. Lots of huge organizations license ideas.

- Develop a Prototype and Test It. If you decide to manufacture the product by yourself, you will require a prototype or sample to ensure the product can be manufactured using your chosen specs. Various experts have different opinions about this step. Here, you may make numerous adjustments, and it might take some months to finish up.

- Secure Intellectual Property. You may also desire to secure your intellectual property. To do this, you can purchase a trademark or register for a patent. You can equally get a copyright for your product idea.

Your task would be less complicated if you sort out these before picking a factory. The instant you provide solutions to those questions, you are ready to create your product.

Where to Find and Contact Manufacturers

There are two methods of locating manufacturers. You can either locate them online or meet with them physically.

Physical Meeting

Here, you need to compile a list of possible manufacturers and visit them. This is easy to do if you are deciding to go with a domestic manufacturer. But, if you possess the means, you can check out manufacturers situated overseas.

For example, if you are aiming to target China, then your best bet would be to look at the Conton Fair for imports and exports situated in China. It lets you physically meet with manufacturers situated in China. You will be able to meet as much as you want daily and get their contact information without the need to make any call. There are equally a lot of fairs which allow you to do this.

The major benefit you get from approaching manufacturers physically is that you would have the chance to pay a visit to their factory. You will also have the chance of seeing how they produce the products, verify the quality of the product, and develop a rapport with the manufacturer. The drawback to this method, however, is that it can require a bit of cash and time.

Tips for Searching

- Find manufacturers who would be able to produce the kind of product you desire.

- Establish a list of choices.

- Create questions to ask the producers.

- Arrange meetings.

- Meet with manufactures, have a look around their facilities and ask questions.

Approaching Manufactures Online

If meeting manufacturers physically would not be an excellent idea for you, you will be able to look for one online. The significance of this method is that it consumes less time and money. On the downside, you would be unable to see the production quality in a person. However, you can use the available technology this approach has to offer. For instance, a Skype or Live meeting solution can aid you in seeing who you are speaking to and develop a relationship.

Finding Manufacturers Online

There are a lot of tools available which you can utilize in locating manufactures online. There are open sites available like Alibaba, Global Sources, and AliExpress. However, these websites have lots of manufacturing fraud. For a more secure option, you can try out Sourcify. You can equally do a quick search on Instagram for manufacturers if you can get a hold of their usernames. This way, you can take a look at some of their prior creations before deciding to use their services.

Outreach

There are numerous manufacturers available producing amazing products. Don't be scared about doing some outreach. Check out LinkedIn, and you are certainly going to find some great sources you can reach out to.

When making an outreach, ensure you don't write a mail which is too lengthy and hard to read. The more detail you add, the less probability of you getting a response. Be sure to provide the manufacturer with a comprehensive description of what you desire from the email.

If you need to make payment for a sample and have it produced, let it be clearly stated.

Using Platforms in Your Ads to Leverage and Sell Your Product

Recently, Instagram included a shopping feature. With this feature, brands are able to include shoppable, sponsored content in their posts. When clients shop for a precise item, they generally consider numerous kinds before they make a purchase.

Displaying a product using images is the best method of swaying a customer who is checking out their options. Sponsored Instagram posts will also give brands the capacity to place their products in the feeds of prospective clients.

Sponsored posts are not as intrusive as using an email newsletter. This is because marketing is incorporated into Instagram.

Doing this is not difficult. All you need to do is:

- Note well-known products in your store which you can take videos and pictures.

- Link your Shopify Account or other similar accounts with your Instagram account.

- Tag your products in your videos and images, then link them directly to the page where you are selling the product.

- Observe as customers troop to your store.

Chapter 9:
Different Ways to Make Money on Instagram

Social media platforms have continued to develop rapidly. For this reason, lots of individuals have begun to make a living from the platform. Now being an influencer on Instagram is a career.

One similar thing Instagram influencers share is reaching. With adequate reach, lots of brands and organizations pay influencers lots of money to post about services or products to get to those followers. Influencers are also usually focused on one niche. They either make posts on food, fashion, technology, or travel. This sort of focus is appealing to brands because they can get to a particular audience.

So how exactly do you earn cash from Instagram even if you do not have a massive amount of followers? Well, that is what we will be covering in this chapter. But before we move any further, below are a few things you have to do to aid your profile in making the cut.

Types of Profile That Earn Cash on Instagram

Irrespective of the method they decide to use in earning cash on Instagram, profiles that do earn cash have some things in common. Some of these include:

Focus

Brands do not want to reach all individuals. They have a precise audience they are after. The audience includes individuals that tend to purchase their products. A footwear brand will contact influencers because they post about stuff related to fashion.

Begin by focusing on a specific niche so followers and brands would know what to look forward to when they head to your page. Take a look at the things already on your profile to determine the things you have a passion for.

A focus should not be too broad. It should be large enough to develop a precise audience; however, it should not be too narrow that you would be unable to develop a huge follower base.

Style

Most pages have a precise style that offers their profile a consistent look. Perhaps it is the kind of colors and photos. It could also be the kind of caption. Irrespective of what you decide to go with, find what makes your images and videos unique and work with that.

Visuals

Instagram is a social network based on images. You can't work around this. If you do not have a way to provide amazing images, you might not find it easy. While it is essential to have great pictures on your feed, you don't have to invest in expensive equipment at the start. You can begin with a decent phone camera, then move up to a dedicated camera after you have built up your audience.

A Great Profile

Instagram has a decent level of engagement. That is why it is one of the best platforms to become an influencer. However, if you annoy your followers, you will most likely lose their interest. Ensure you do not post only sponsored posts; no one will follow you only to see adverts.

Ensure you strike a balance using the images and videos that initially helped you in getting followers. Also, ensure you don't vanish for a huge amount of days without explanation. You need to post regularly.

How to Make Money on Instagram

Instagram is a known platform for the operation of various kind of businesses. Instagram is widely used by different persons, businesses, and companies, be it big companies or small companies or persons who make use of the platform as a side job. There are different alternate ways one can earn money on Instagram, which are:

Become an Influencer

An influencer is a recognized person within a sphere of life. This person is respected and considered a sort of authority by his/her followers. An influencer could be anybody: a blogger, an activist, a social accolyte, an actor/actress, a business guru, or a makeup artist.

It is, however, essential to have gained stable and constant followers and viewers who connected to your personality, lifestyle, and what you generally represent. To promote their brands and products, companies and business owners can engage the services of influencers for the sake of advertisement. The job description of the influencer is to derive creative ways and methods to portray the products of a company, either through pictures, videos, or voice.

You can choose to be an influencer and help drive sales indirectly to your business.

As an influencer, you must be aware of the various communities open and available to you. The advantage of these communities is to create a general database, with the aim of easy accessibility of influencers by these companies, businesses, or persons who need their services. Find below the influencer communities that can be taken into account:

- Ifluenz: This is a platform where influencers register their proposals with various brands or companies. The latter can shortlist the type of influencers they desire to represent their product or brand. One of the significant requirements you must meet is to have at least 5000 followers. The platform provides for sales of influencer's pictures without necessarily reaching out to them.

- Shout Cart: This application is built like an online store. The influencer is required to create a profile on their specialty. Companies and brands are then presented with various choices of influencers to pick from. It is crucial that their profile entails prices or specification on the type of campaign they engage in; if a campaign represents what you don't stand for or is not tailored to what your audience expects, you have the option of rejecting the employment.

- Popular Pays: This platform is otherwise called "let the best man win." On this platform, companies post their ideas about the type of campaign they want to project. Influencers registered with Popular Pays then create a creative pitch that represents what the brand stands for or expects from them. The best job is first approved, and the influencer chosen is paid.

- Tribe Group: This platform is unique compared to others. It sets the interest of the influencer above anything else. They post the amount they are expected to be paid for the job done. The platform also gives the influencers the opportunity to be creative and unique without been limited to the expectations of brands and companies. The disadvantage is the application is limited to Australia.

- Heartbeat: This platform is mostly centered on female influencers without necessarily having large numbers of followers. The influencers are required to state their preferences on what kind of brands they desire to work with and who they are; this data is used to match the best-suited brands in need of their services. The monetary terms are, however, on the low size, and sometimes a consideration for services rendered are free products.

Market Your Product

Sometimes you are not limited to promoting other people's product. If you also produce your own items, this is the best opportunity to share them with your followers on Instagram. All you need to do is create space where you can store these products. You might want to engage the services of a delivering company that can assist in sending out your products. You must note that for you to be successful in this, you must be serious, consistent, and accountable. With some planning and startup capital, you are good to go.

Sales of Artwork

Instagram is the perfect platform to use in engaging your followers who love artwork. The sale of artwork does not come in the intangible sizes as displayed on your phone. The application called 8x10 can translate your work into frames that can be hung on a wall. 8x10 provides for the processes of sales from start to finish, such as the printing out of the pictures, the framing, the delivering, and the payment made. All you have to do is create a unique or impressive piece you desire to put to the market. The application will then develop a sample that can be used for advertisement on your Instagram page. You can advertise this sample on different platforms, on the 8x10 app, your website, or Instagram. Once a sale is made, 8x10 gets a commission out of the sale, and the rest is sent to you. The peak of this application is that the artist gets to decide how much he/she wants to sell his/her work. If a sale is not made, then payment is not made.

Stock Photography

Stock photography is a great way to make money on Instagram, especially if you are great at taking pictures. These pictures can be sold to different companies. However, when selling to these companies, it is advisable to read their licensing agreements and their terms and conditions, to make sure you do not violate or breach any of their requirements. It is also essential to verify the size and kind of picture that is acceptable.

This is because some companies do not accept Instagram sized pictures. You can, however, look up companies like Twenty20 and Foap. These companies pride themselves in gathering or purchasing authentic and creative photos from talented photographers. This opportunity is, however, not restricted to pictures that are Instagram friendly. You can find an alternate way of selling pictures of other stock companies from way back, such as Getty, Shutterstock, and the like.

Utilize Instagram to Enhance Your Income on YouTube

This is perfect if you operate more than one social media account, such as Instagram, LinkedIn, Facebook, YouTube, and your official website. Each of these platforms has its strength and weaknesses. The best way to complement these accounts is by exploring their strengths to your advantage.

For example, LinkedIn is ideal for professionals; it is best to do your presentation with words, while Instagram is photo oriented. Unlike the limitations on Instagram, YouTube gives unlimited access to create unique content, while Facebook presents an audience of billions. The more audience you have, the more followers you have, and you will be considered as an influencer or one with a capacity to affiliate with a company. It is then vital to wisely maximize every platform at your disposal.

Become an Affiliate

There are numerous opportunities available to you if you are willing to affiliate with companies or businesses. All you have to do is to derive creative ways to market these companies' products online and receive a commission for each sale.

One of the most feared possibilities is the inability to trace sales made. This should not be a worry as there is a link to trace sales made through the marketer on Instagram. You can also use a code to decipher sales made. Unfortunately, Instagram allows only one link access, and as a result, you cannot create a link on each post you upload.

You can, however, refer your potential customer to your bio, to click on the available link and purchase their desired product. There are differences between a salesperson, who is affiliated with a company, and an influencer. A salesperson gets paid only when a product is sold through commission, while an influencer advertises products and get paid for it.

To be an affiliate or salesperson, you must apply strategic methods to market your products without seeming persistent. Once you come off as being forceful, followers are likely to lose interest, and at worst unfollow you. To create a broader reach, you can explore other social media platform to complement your Instagram pages, such as Twitter, Facebook, or LinkedIn. This way, you can successfully grow your clients.

Attain Sponsorship

One unique feature of Instagram is its special plugins created for business pages and business owners. As a result of this, you can sponsor a post. Influencers are best known to utilize this adequately. As an influencer, you can make use of these sponsored post on behalf of companies your brands. As an influencer, you do not want to saturate your display content on just advertised products. This will result in you losing your authentic self and creativity, and as a result, you might lose your followers and your true self. It is better you maintain who you truly are. When you find the brand you desire to work, create a beautiful content that naturally attracts your audience without you seemingly forcing a product on them. As a general rule on Instagram, post 80% original content and 20% of advertisement. Make sure that for every promotional post you upload, post four of your own content. This way, you still maintain your core values while making money.

Finding Sponsors

Sometimes you don't have to wait for companies to approach you before you make your interest known. If you are interested in the core values of a company and its product, you can pitch your ideas on a campaign. When doing this, highlight your strengths through your contents and send a sample on how you intend to publicize their products. An alternative approach is to join an influencer community or register with an agent that can watch out for your best interest.

Dropshipping

You can earn money from Instagram by acting as a middleman or an intermediary. Dropshipping occurs when you deliver a product directly from your supplier's store to your customer's address. This way, you do not have to keep inventory. You do not also concern yourself with the storage mechanism or shipping process. You act as an agent and earn your money. And this can be perfectly mastered on Instagram. You wouldn't need start-up capital or an inventory. Different e-commerce platforms can be maximized in practicing the act of dropshipping, such as Oberlo or Shopify.

Selling of Accounts

It is sometimes the common practice where an Instagram user builds his/her account to a great capacity, such as having a large number of followers and has contracts with brands and companies but sells off this account. This can be done through mediums like viral accounts. The sale of this kind account can bring a lot of money and can be considered excellent business, especially if the account has a high followers count. Although this process takes time, patience, and hard work, it is very profitable.

Conclusion

Instagram is not just a tool to show some great pictures and let the audience know how incredible your content is. There is a reason why the biggest brands in the world - from Coca-Cola to Unilever to Mercedes-Benz - are on the platform. They know the potential of Instagram. They understand the appeal it has to people.

Within just the past two years, Instagram has gained so much strength not just for individuals, but for marketers as well. It has been estimated that people spend at least 53 minutes a day on the app!

53 minutes!

Imagine the potential of that fact.

Instagram knows this. This is why it is offering a variety of tools for businesses in order for them to use the platform and promote their products. No matter what size your business is, you can thrive on the platform.

Are you a mom-and-pop store? Sure, get on the platform and start getting some fans and customers. Are you a big brand? Well, I don't have to show you the examples of brands already finding Instagram profitable.

The flexibility and features that you gain from Instagram are nearly unparalleled. And to think that everything is free unless you decide to spend a little more, which is also entirely based on your business decision!

So, I hope you have gained some valuable insights into

Instagram and are prepared to give your business the social media boost it requires.

#TimeToGoBig

References

Getting started on Instagram for businesses. (2019). Retrieved from https://business.instagram.com/getting-started

Ivanov, Ivan. (2017). How to Build a Brand Personality That Resonates on Instagram. Retrieved from https://www.business2community.com/instagram/build-brand-personality-resonates-instagram-01926567

Wade, Jessica. (2018). 20 Instagram statistics every marketer should know about for 2018. Retrieved from https://www.smartinsights.com/social-media-marketing/instagram-marketing/instagram-statistics/ .

Loechner, J. (2019). 60% Of Apparel Retailers On Five Social Channels; 86% On Four. Retrieved from http://www.mediapost.com/publications/article/252909/60-of-apparel-retailers-on-five-social-channels.html

The 15 Best Instagram Marketing Campaigns of 2017. (2019). Retrieved from https://www.wordstream.com/blog/ws/2017/03/24/best-instagram-marketing-campaigns

Worthy, Page. (2018). Top Instagram Demographics That Matter to Social Media Marketers. Retrieved from https://blog.hootsuite.com/instagram-demographics/

D'innocenzio, Anne. (2018). Walmart's online same-day grocery ready for prime-time. Retrieved from https://www.marketbeat.com/articles/walmarts-online-same-day-grocery-ready-for-prime-time-2018-03-13/

Who Are Millennials | Millennial Marketing. (2019). Retrieved from
http://www.millennialmarketing.com/who-are-millennials/

5 Most Significant Instagram Benefits for Business Marketing.
(2016). Retrieved from
https://www.yotpo.com/blog/instagram-pics-better/

Why We're More Likely To Remember Content With Images And
Video (Infographic). (2014). Retrieved from
https://www.fastcompany.com/3035856/why-were-more-likely-t
o-remember-content-with-images-and-video-infogr

Kolowich, L. (2019). The Ultimate List of Instagram Stats [2019].
Retrieved from
https://blog.hubspot.com/marketing/instagram-stats

Top Ten Benefits of Using Instagram For Your Business (Part I).
(2018). Retrieved from
https://medium.com/@turngram/top-ten-benefits-of-using-instag
ram-for-your-business-part-i-763d90c16808

Dholakiya, P. (2016). 6 Ways to Convert Your Instagram Audience
into Customers. Retrieved from
https://www.entrepreneur.com/article/285674